WRESTLING STRENGTH

DARE TO EXCEL

Matt Brzycki

a RAM Publishing Pruduction
Blue River Press, Indianapolis, Indiana

LCCN: 2004105883

Cover designed by Phil Velikan
Cover photography courtesy of Lanny Bryant, *Wrestling USA* magazine

Printed in the United States of America
10 9 8 7 6 5 4 3 2 1

Distributed in the United States by
Cardinal Publishers Group
7301 Georgetown Road, Suite 118
Indianapolis, Indiana 46268
www.cardinalpub.com

TABLE OF CONTENTS

PREFACE

From February 1986 - May 2004, I have had nearly 80 articles featured in *Wrestling USA* magazine. I would like to thank Lanny Bryant and his family for publishing those articles in their magazine and granting permission to allow them to be compiled in book form.

The articles were written over the course of more than 18 years, the earliest appearing in the February 15, 1986 issue. I have done some editing of the articles for this book to "standardize" the changes in my style of writing that have occurred over this lengthy period of time. Actually, all of the articles that I wrote prior to 1991 were done on a typewriter. As you might imagine, it was quite painstaking to make any changes to the text. In fact, making the smallest of changes required retyping sections of the article or, in some cases, the entire article. Needless to say, the texts of those early articles were essentially rough "first drafts" and I have used this opportunity to make belated edits.

Though I never competed as a wrestler, the sport of wrestling has given me a wealth of fond memories. My earliest recollection dates back to when I was a young teen who marveled at – and was inspired by – the renowned physical training of the great Dan Gable as he prepared for the 1972 Olympics in Munich. Another memory that I have of wrestlers is from 1978. At the time, I was a 21-year-old Drill Instructor at the Marine Corps Recruit Depot in San Diego, California. As part of their training, recruits had to maneuver through an obstacle course that consisted of numerous poles, logs, beams and hurdles and ended with a rope climb. Negotiating the obstacle course in a speedy fashion requires a high degree of strength, balance, agility and determination. As motivation, recruits were timed in their efforts and a record was kept for the best-ever time. Every now and then, a recruit would break the all-time record by a half second or so. One day, word quickly spread about a recruit who broke the record for the obstacle course by an unbelievable two seconds. The depot newspaper ran an article about the recruit who set the new record – an unusually large individual who had gone to college on a football scholarship and later joined the Marines. To make a long story short, the recruit was Greg Gibson. He went on to become a three-time world silver medalist in freestyle wrestling from 1981 - 83 and the 1984 Olympic silver medalist in Greco-Roman wrestling. (Greg retired as a Master Sergeant from the Marine Corps in May of 2003 after 23 years of service and is currently assistant coach of the All-Marine Wrestling Team.) In 1981 as an undergraduate student at Penn State, I participated in a wrestling class taught by the legendary Bill Koll who was a three-time NCAA champion for Northern Iowa (1946 - 48) and twice won the award as the outstanding wrestler in the tournament (1947 - 48). Despite his age, we still dreaded having him demonstrate moves on us. Among other things, we did not want to be on the wrong end of a cross face.

Of all the different sports with which I have worked over the years, I have been with wrestling the longest and on the most regular basis. Since September 1982, I have been involved in the strength and conditioning of collegiate wrestlers at three different schools: Penn State, Princeton and Rutgers. Over this period of time, I have met a great number of wrestlers and coaches who have meant much to me both professionally as well as personally. From a professional standpoint, I have had the opportunity to work with two of the all-time coaching greats in the history of collegiate wrestling: John Johnston of Princeton and Deane Oliver of Rutgers – both of whom were head coaches at the collegiate level for a total of more than a half century (and they themselves were accomplished collegiate wrestlers as well). In addition, I have worked with hundreds of their wrestlers (and those of John Johnston's two very capable coaching successors, Eric Pearson and Michael New) who are far too numerous to mention. From a personal standpoint, the best man at my wedding was Andy Foltiny who wrestled for Rutgers in the late 1970s (captaining the team as a senior) and then served as an assistant wrestling coach at the school for more than a decade. Andy was also my training partner from 1985 - 90 and, pound-for-pound, was one of the strongest men that I have ever seen. And several years ago, Tom O'Rourke – another exceptionally strong individual who wrestled for Andy at Rutgers (also captaining the team as a senior) – asked me to be the godfather of his daughter, Kathleen.

Wrestlers quickly gained my utmost respect primarily because of their warrior-like nature. Like true warriors, wrestlers are generally fierce, relentless, intense, aggressive, dedicated, resourceful and purposeful to a degree that separates them from most others. Boxers, judo players and the various martial artists are also true warriors. Unfortunately, the fact of the matter is that the warrior is a vanishing breed.

As a sport, you cannot get much more basic than wrestling. There is really no equipment except for the uniform – and there is very little of that. There are no implements or apparatus. It is just a wrestler and an opponent. Two warriors. One goal.

This book is dedicated to wrestlers and the warrior lifestyle.

Matt Brzycki
May 2, 2004

Chapter 1

BASIC TRAINING FOR WRESTLING: THE ESSENTIALS

In the military, basic training is meant to provide a basic knowledge of the essentials that are necessary to function effectively in a particular branch of service. For the most part, the foundations that are established in basic training prepare an individual for the future.

In wrestling, a basic knowledge of essentials is also necessary to establish a foundation for the future. In this case, the essentials will prepare you for the rigors of wrestling. The sport of wrestling involves a unique blend of muscular strength, cardiovascular conditioning, flexibility and technical expertise. Preparation for wrestling, then, must include specific activities that develop these essentials.

THE ESSENTIAL COMPONENTS

The following information is meant to provide you with a brief outline of the essential components of basic training that are necessary for your physical preparedness as a wrestler.

Strength Training

There is no consensus as to the optimal way of developing muscular strength. Nor is there any shortage of opinions. The fact of the matter is that many programs – despite being, in some cases, polar opposites – can be effective. A strength-training program for wrestling will produce desirable results if it incorporates these basic guidelines:

- Exercise with an appropriate degree of intensity (or effort).

- Try to progress from one workout to the next by either increasing the amount of resistance that you used or improving upon the number of repetitions that you did with the same resistance.
- Avoid doing the repetitions with an excessive amount of momentum.
- Perform each repetition throughout a full range of motion.
- Focus on the larger muscle groups in your body (hips, legs and torso).
- Strengthen your neck as a safeguard against traumatic injury.
- Exercise your muscles from largest to smallest (hips, upper legs, lower legs, torso, upper arms, lower arms, abdominals and lower back).
- Take as little rest as possible between exercises/sets.
- Allow for adequate recovery between workouts.
- Keep track of your performances in the weight room (resistance and repetitions).
- Train with a partner.

Conditioning

Proper conditioning for wrestling should involve aerobic and anaerobic training. You can improve your conditioning for wrestling by following these basics:

- Focus on aerobic conditioning – that is, continuous efforts of long duration such as long-distance running – to establish a solid foundation of aerobic support.
- Concentrate on anaerobic conditioning – that is, a series of all-out efforts of short duration such as sprints – as your competitive season nears.
- Elevate your heart rate to levels that will stimulate a training response.
- Try to progress from one workout to the next by completing the same distance at a faster pace (in a shorter amount of time), covering a greater distance at the same pace or gradually increasing both the distance and the

pace.
- Include some non-weightbearing activities in your training – such as swimming and rowing – to reduce your risk of experiencing or complicating an orthopedic problem.

Flexibility

By becoming more flexible, you have increased the ranges of motion around your joints. Among other things, this gives you the potential to apply force over a greater distance. A flexibility program for wrestling will be effective if it implements these basic guidelines:
- Precede your flexibility training with a warm-up that causes you to break a light sweat.
- Do the stretch under control without any bouncing, bobbing or jerking movements.
- Inhale and exhale normally during the stretch without holding your breath.
- Stretch comfortably in a pain-free manner.
- Relax during the stretch.
- Hold each stretch for about 30 - 60 seconds.
- Attempt to stretch a little bit farther than the last time.
- Stretch all of the major muscle groups in your body.
- Perform flexibility movements on a regular basis.

Skill Training

The most essential component of your basic training is the learning and perfecting of your wrestling techniques. You will develop your wrestling skills if you adhere to the following basic guidelines:
- Learn how to do your skills correctly.
- Perform your skills over and over again until you can execute them without conscious effort.
- Practice your skills perfectly and exactly as you would use them on the mat.
- Avoid trying to simulate wrestling skills with barbells, dumbbells or other weighted equipment.

BACK TO BASICS

Individuals are often intrigued by training methods that sound exotic or are touted as a "secret." In many instances, they believe that training must be complicated or elaborate in order to be effective. But productive training can actually be quite simple and very basic.

An understanding of the basics is not just for beginning wrestlers. Even seasoned grapplers will be better prepared for competition if they learn and implement the essential components of basic training for wrestling.

Chapter 2

FACTORS THAT DETERMINE STRENGTH POTENTIAL

Have you ever noticed that some wrestlers make striking gains in strength while others make only modest ones – even though all of them may be performing the identical program in the weight room (that is, the same exercises using the same number of sets and repetitions)? In some cases, different responses to training may be the result of exercising with different levels of intensity. Most of the variations in the response to training, however, are primarily the result of an individual's genetic (or inherited) characteristics. Except for identical twins, each person is a unique genetic entity with a different strength potential.

GENETIC FACTORS

A number of genetic factors play a major role in determining your strength potential. These include the following:

Muscle-Fiber Type

One of the most influential of all genetic factors is your muscle-fiber type. Your muscle fibers can be categorized as slow twitch (ST) or Type I and fast twitch (FT) or Type II. From a functional standpoint, muscle fibers differ in a number of ways including speed of contraction, magnitude of force and degree of fatigability.

Most muscles have a blend of about 50% ST fibers and 50% FT fibers. (The fibers are intermingled throughout each muscle.) Some wrestlers, however, inherit a greater proportion of one fiber type that influences their strength potential. Due to their larger diameter, FT fibers produce greater force than ST fibers. Everything else being equal, wrestlers who have high percentages of FT fibers have a greater potential to improve their strength than others who have low percentages of FT fibers. It should also be noted that a wrestler's fiber-type mixture can vary from one muscle to another and may even vary from one side of the body to the other.

Incidentally, there is no scientific evidence that consistently and convincingly supports the notion that ST fibers can be converted into FT fibers or vice versa. It appears as if one type of muscle fiber may take on certain metabolic characteristics of another type but actual conversion does not occur. Stated differently, you cannot convert one fiber type into another any more than you can convert lead into gold.

While on the subject, an increase in the number of muscle fibers – known as "hyperplasia" – is thought to take place by fiber splitting or "budding." Although hyperplasia has been demonstrated scientifically in many animals whose muscles were loaded with a resistance – including birds, cats and rats – there is no definitive proof that it occurs in humans. Most likely, strength training results in the addition of contractile protein – namely, actin and myosin – not in the addition of muscle fibers.

Muscle-to-Tendon Ratio

Another factor that determines strength potential is the relationship or ratio between the length of a muscle and the length of its tendon. The potential for a muscle to increase in size (or hypertrophy) is directly related to its length. Everything else being equal, wrestlers who have long muscles and short tendons have a greater potential for achieving muscular size than others who have short muscles and long tendons.

But how does this relate to strength potential? Well, a bigger muscle has a larger cross-sectional area. A larger cross-sectional area contains a greater number of protein filaments (actin and myosin) and crossbridges, thereby increasing its capacity to produce force. Therefore, a *bigger* muscle – in terms of its cross-sectional area – is also a *stronger* muscle. This means that wrestlers with long muscles have the potential to be quite strong. Understand, too, that a small variation in the length of a muscle makes a considerable difference in strength (and size) potential.

As with muscle-fiber type, a wrestler's muscle-to-tendon ratio can vary from one muscle to another. It is difficult to determine the actual length of a muscle because it may be hidden by subcutaneous fat (the fat between a muscle and the skin) or lie beneath other muscles. However, the lengths of the triceps, the forearms and especially the calves are usually easy to identify. The lengths of a muscle and its tendon are not subject to change.

Testosterone Level

Although it is a male sex hormone, testosterone is also found in the blood of perfectly normal women. In men, testosterone is produced by the testes; in women, roughly 50% is produced by the ovaries and 50% by the adrenal glands. The secretion of testosterone is regulated by pituitary hormones.

Testosterone influences the secondary sexual characteristics. In men, for example, it lowers the pitch of the voice and is associated with the growth of facial hair and, inexplicably, male pattern baldness. Additionally, testosterone stimulates skeletal growth as well as increases in muscle mass and strength. In short, its major action is to promote growth. Everything else being equal, wrestlers who have high levels of testosterone have a greater potential to improve their strength than others who have low levels of testosterone.

Interestingly, a number of studies have also found a correlation between testosterone levels and aggressive behavior in both men and women. This is not unique in the animal kingdom, by the way. Bull sharks have the highest levels of testosterone found in any creature (land or sea) and their aggressive behavior is legendary. It is, perhaps, the most dangerous type of shark in the world.

Lever Lengths and Body Proportions

Some wrestlers have lever (bone) lengths and body proportions that give them greater leverage in the weight room and a greater strength potential than other wrestlers. For instance, those who are most successful in the bench press tend to have relatively short arms and thick chests. Everything else being equal, wrestlers with those lever lengths and body proportions have a greater strength potential in most pushing and pulling movements because they do not have to move the weight as far as others who have less favorable characteristics. Likewise, those who are most successful in the squat tend to have short torsos, thick abdomens, wide hips and short legs. Everything else being equal, wrestlers with those lever lengths and body proportions have a greater strength potential in squatting and deadlifting movements because they do not have to move the weight as far as others who have less favorable characteristics.

To illustrate, consider two wrestlers who are tasked with lifting 200 pounds in the bench press. Because of lever lengths and body proportions, suppose that Wrestler A has to move the weight a distance of 20 inches and Wrestler B has to move the weight 22 inches. Since "work" is defined as "force [or weight] times distance," Wrestler A must do 4,000 inch-pounds of work [20 inches x 200 pounds] and Wrestler B must do 4,400 inch-pounds of work [22 inches x 200 pounds] to accomplish the same task. In other words, Wrestler A does not need to make anywhere near as much effort as Wrestler B to lift the weight. Wrestler A would have greater leverage than Wrestler B and, everything else being equal, would have a greater strength potential.

Body Type

Another genetic factor that plays a critical role in strength potential is a wrestler's body type or somatotype. In the 1940s, Dr. William H. Sheldon – a physician and psychologist – proposed that there are three main body types: endomorph, mesomorph and ectomorph. Endomorphs are characterized by softness and round physiques. They have high percentages of body fat and very little muscle tone. A sumo wrestler is a classic example of an endomorph. Mesomorphs are typified by heavily muscled physiques. They have athletic builds with broad shoulders, large chests and slender waists. A competitive bodybuilder is a classic example of a mesomorph. Finally, ectomorphs are characterized by long limbs, leanness and slender physiques. They have low percentages of body fat but also little in the way of muscular size. A successful long-distance runner is a classic example of an ectomorph.

Since almost everyone has some degree of each component, various rating systems were developed in which an individual is given a "score" in each of the three areas. The system that was developed by Dr. Sheldon introduced a scale that ranged from 1 to 7 to designate the degree of each of the three components with 1 being the least amount and 7 being the greatest. In his system, a somatotype of 7-1-1 indicates extreme endomorphy (fatness), 1-7-1 extreme mesomorphy (muscularity) and 1-1-7 extreme ectomorphy (leanness).

Relatively few wrestlers can be classified as being purely one body type or another. Although wrestlers have a tendency toward one body type, most are a combination of two types. For example, a wrestler who has a somatotype of 1-4-4 would have a slender physique, a low percentage of body fat and a high degree of muscular development and be characterized as an ecto-mesomorph; a wrestler who has a somatotype of 4-4-1 would have a round physique, a high percentage of body fat and a high degree of muscular development and be characterized as an endo-mesomorph.

A number of studies have related body type to physical performance. As you might suspect, the body type that has the greatest strength potential is the mesomorph. Everything else being equal, wrestlers who have high degrees of mesomorphy have a greater potential to improve their strength than others who have low degrees of mesomorphy. (A study of athletes who competed in the 1968 Olympics found that the average somatotype of a wrestler was 2.2-6.3-1.6, indicating a high degree of mesomorphy.)

Tendon Insertions

At one time or another, you probably encountered wrestlers who were far stronger on the mat than they appeared. In fact, they may have been incredibly strong despite not having much in the way of muscular size. How is this possible if muscular strength is directly related to muscular size (in terms of cross-sectional area)? One possible reason is that the wrestlers may have favorable points of tendon insertions. The fact of the matter is that the farther away a tendon inserts from an axis of rotation the greater the biomechanical advantage and strength potential.

Consider two wrestlers who are tasked with holding 100 pounds a distance of 12.0 inches from their elbows while keeping their lower arms parallel to the ground and maintaining a 90-degree angle between their upper and lower arms. Suppose that Wrestler A has a bicep tendon that inserts on the forearm 1.2 inches from the elbow and Wrestler B has a bicep tendon that inserts on the forearm 1.0 inch from the elbow. In this example, the force necessary to maintain the weight (or resistance) in a static position can be calculated by using this formula: "force times force arm equals resistance times resistance arm" or, more simply, "F x FA = R x RA." The force arm is defined as "the distance from the axis of rotation [in this case, the elbow] to the point where the force is applied" (the insertion point of the tendon); the resistance arm is defined as "the distance from the axis of rotation to the point where the resistance is applied." Inserting the previously given values into the formula reveals that Wrestler A must produce 1,000 pounds of force to hold the 100-pound weight in a static position while Wrestler B must produce 1,200 pounds of force to accomplish the same task. In other words, Wrestler A does not need to make anywhere near as much effort as Wrestler B to hold the weight. Wrestler A would have greater leverage than Wrestler B and, everything else being equal, would have a greater strength potential.

This depiction of static forces is somewhat simplified. However, it still illustrates the fact that a very small difference in the insertion point of a tendon can make a considerable amount of variation in leverage. Magnetic resonance imaging (MRI) and X-rays can be used to accurately determine the insertion points of tendons.

Neurological Efficiency

One more genetic factor that has a role in determining strength potential deals with the nervous system and has been termed "neurological (or neuromuscular) efficiency." This refers to an individual's inherited ability to recruit (or innervate) muscle fibers and is another reason why some wrestlers may be far stronger than they appear. It has been suggested that some individuals can recruit high percentages of their muscle fibers which gives them a greater potential to improve their strength than others who can recruit low percentages of their muscle fibers.

Consider two wrestlers who have the same amount of muscle mass. Suppose that Wrestler A can recruit 40% of his muscle fibers and Wrestler B can recruit 30%. Wrestler A would be able to access a higher percentage of muscle fibers than Wrestler B and, everything else being equal, would have a have a greater strength potential.

HERITABILITY VERSUS TRAINABILITY

With all due respect to Abraham Lincoln, all wrestlers are not created equal. If two wrestlers use the exact same method of training, it is highly unlikely that they will end up having the exact same level of strength. Each wrestler responds in a different manner because – except for identical twins – each wrestler has a different potential for improving strength. Simply, some wrestlers are predisposed toward developing high levels of strength while others are not.

So, your response to training is not necessarily due to a particular program or routine. Indeed, following the routines of successful weightlifters does not mean that you will attain their same levels of strength. Think about this analogy: If you were to train a racehorse like a draft horse, you might get a slightly stronger racehorse but you will never get a draft horse. The next time that you are in the weight room, observe different pairs of training partners. You will see that wrestlers who work out together usually have different levels of strength (and size) – despite doing the same exercises while using the same number of sets and repetitions.

The truth is that heritability dictates trainability. Your response to training is largely determined by your genetic characteristics. The cumulative effect of your inherited muscular, mechanical, hormonal and neural qualities is what determines your strength potential. A wrestler who has a high percentage of FT fibers, long muscles coupled with short tendons, high levels of testosterone, favorable lever lengths and body proportions, a high degree of mesomorphy, low points of tendon insertions and an efficient neurological system would be incredibly strong (as well as physically impressive). Compared to the average person, this genetic marvel would be capable of almost unbelievable feats of strength. There are some wrestlers like that but most are not as fortunate.

For all intents and purposes, you cannot change the characteristics that you have inherited from your ancestors. But this does not mean that you cannot get stronger. Regardless of your genetic destiny, your goal should be to realize your strength potential.

Chapter 3

HOW MANY SETS?

For many years, most people have done multiple-set training simply because that is what they have read or been told to do. The roots of this advice can be traced back to the time when virtually every authority in strength training came from the ranks of the professional strongmen, competitive weightlifters and, to a lesser degree, bodybuilders. In the early 1970s, the notion was advanced that people could improve their muscular strength (and size) with far fewer sets – and, thus, less volume of training – than had been traditionally thought. The debate concerning the ideal number of sets has been raging ever since.

THE SCIENTIFIC PERSPECTIVE

Know this: Science has been unable to determine how many sets of each exercise are necessary to produce optimal increases in muscular strength (and size). But the overwhelming majority of scientific evidence indicates that single-set training is at least as effective as multiple-set training. An exhaustive literature review in 1998 by Drs. Ralph Carpinelli and Robert Otto of Adelphi University (New York) and later reviews by Dr. Carpinelli examined all studies that compared different numbers of sets (dating back to 1956). Collectively, their research found 5 studies that showed multiple-set training was superior to single-set training *and 57 that did not*. Two of the five studies that concluded multiple-set training was superior to single-set training involved only one exercise. One of these studies was done in 1962 and used only the bench press; the other study only reported data from the barbell squat. (Curiously, there were five other exercises used in the latter study but no data were reported for them.)

THE EMPIRICAL PERSPECTIVE

So, the basis for performing single-set training – or a relatively low number of sets – has powerful and compelling support in the scientific literature. But is single-set training actually done in the "real world"? More importantly, can "experienced" or "trained" athletes obtain the same results from single-set training as they can from multiple-set training? The answer to both questions is "yes." The fact of the matter is that single-set training has been popular since the early 1970s. And to quote Drs. Carpinelli and Otto: "There is no evidence to suggest that the response to single or multiple sets in trained athletes would differ from that in untrained individuals." Indeed, numerous authorities advocate single-set training including the strength coaches for many collegiate and professional teams. Dan Riley – a veteran strength coach with more than 20 years of experience in the National Football League and another 8 at the collegiate level (Penn State and Army) – notes, "Your goal must be to perform as few sets as possible while stimulating maximum gains. If performed properly, only one set is needed to generate maximum gains. In our standard routines, one set of each exercise is performed."

OVERLOAD: THE KEY

In order for your muscles to increase in strength (and size), they must experience an adequate level of fatigue. It is just that simple. It really does not matter whether your muscles are fatigued in one set or several sets – as long as you produce a sufficient level of fatigue.

Despite the overwhelming scientific and empirical evidence pointing to the effectiveness single-set training, the notion is often met with some degree of skepticism. Having been inundated with information suggesting that "more is better," athletes have difficulty believing that they can increase their muscular size and strength from workouts involving one set of each exercise. Single-set training can indeed be quite productive and very economical in terms of time. However, you simply cannot lift any random resistance and stop at a predetermined number of repetitions. In order for this type of training to be effective, each exercise in your workout must be done to the point of muscular fatigue.

How is an adequate level of fatigue produced in one set? Let us say that you are to perform a set of the tricep extension with 60 pounds. In order to overcome inertia and provide impetus to the 60 pounds of resistance, your triceps must exert slightly more than 60 pounds of force. The weight will not move if you apply a force that is less than or equal to 60 pounds. During the first repetition, only a small percentage of your available muscle fibers is being worked – just enough to move the weight. As you perform each repetition, some muscle fibers will fatigue and will no longer be able to keep up with the increasing metabolic demands. Fresh fibers are simultaneously recruited to assist the fatigued fibers in generating ample force. This continues until the last repetition, when you finally reach muscular fatigue. At this point, your available muscle fibers cannot collectively produce enough force to raise the weight. During this final repetition, the cumulative effect of each preceding repetition has fatigued your triceps thereby providing a very sufficient – and efficient – stimulus for muscular growth.

By performing one set with maximal effort, you have done the equivalent of a few sub-maximal sets . . . but in a shorter amount of time. So one set of an exercise performed in a high-intensity fashion is just as productive as doing multiple sets . . . and obviously more efficient in terms of time.

Remember, too, that a set done in a subsequent workout must be made progressively more challenging by performing more repetitions or increasing the resistance. Suppose, for example, that you did one set of 10 repetitions with 60 pounds in the tricep extension during today's workout. You tried an 11th repetition but were unable to do it. In your next workout, you would again use 60 pounds but try to improve on the 10 repetitions that you did today. Or if your target number of repetitions was 10, you should increase the resistance for your next workout. (Incidentally, when you increase the resistance, your muscles will respond better to smaller improvements – about 5% or less.)

SINGLE VERSUS MULTIPLE SETS

If doing one set of an exercise produces virtually the same results as several sets, then single-set training represents a more efficient means of strength training. After all, why perform several sets when you can obtain similar results from one set in a fraction of the time?

This is not to say that multiple-set training cannot be done. If performed properly, multiple-set training can certainly be effective in overloading your muscles. Multiple-set training has been used successfully by an enormous number of individuals for decades.

If you have a preference for multiple-set training, you should be aware of several things. First of all, simply doing multiple sets does not guarantee that you have overloaded your muscles. If the weights you use are not demanding enough then you will not produce sufficient muscular fatigue and your workout will not be as effective as possible. Remember, a large amount of low-intensity work does not necessarily produce an overload. So if you would rather do multiple sets, make sure that you are challenging your muscles with a progressive overload. In addition, keep in mind that performing too many sets (or too many exercises) can create a situation in which the demands on your muscles have surpassed your ability to recover. If this happens, your muscle tissue will be broken down in such an extreme manner that your body is unable to regenerate muscle tissue (essentially the resynthesis of myofibrillar proteins). Also, doing too many sets (or too many exercises) can significantly increase your risk of incurring an overuse injury such as tendinitis and bursitis. And as was indicated earlier, multiple-set training is relatively inefficient in terms of time so it is undesirable for time-conscious individuals. If you are like most athletes, time is a precious commodity – most of you simply do not have much free time. The point is this: Keep your sets to the minimum amount that is needed to produce an adequate level of muscular fatigue.

To recap: Single-set training can be just as effective as multiple-set training. But again, if a single set of an exercise is to be productive, the set must be done with an appropriate level of intensity – that is, to the point of muscular fatigue. Your muscles should be thoroughly exhausted at the end of each exercise.

MEANINGFUL SETS

You should emphasize the *quality* of work done in the weight room rather than the *quantity* of work. Do not perform meaningless sets in the weight room – make sure that every set is productive and purposeful. The most efficient program is one that produces the *maximum* possible results in the *minimum* amount of time.

Chapter 4

POST-FATIGUE REPETITIONS

If you train to the point of muscular fatigue, you know that it requires a great deal of intensity (or effort). After you have reached muscular fatigue, you can increase the intensity even further by immediately performing several additional post-fatigue (or intensification) repetitions at the end of the set.

BACKGROUND

Before a discussion of post-fatigue repetitions, it is necessary to understand some basic concepts and terminology. Raising a weight is sometimes referred to as the "positive phase" of a repetition and involves a concentric muscular contraction; lowering a weight is occasionally referred to as the "negative phase" of a repetition and involves an eccentric muscular contraction.

Your eccentric (or negative) strength is always greater than your concentric (or positive) strength. Stated differently, you can always lower more resistance than you can raise (in a given exercise). In fact, research has shown that your eccentric strength is about 40% greater than your concentric strength (at least in the case of a fresh muscle). So if you can raise 100 pounds concentrically, you can lower about 140 pounds eccentrically.

Two points can be deduced from this information: First, when you reach muscular fatigue – that is, when you cannot do any more repetitions – it is because your concentric strength has been fatigued to such a degree that you are unable to raise the resistance. Second, although you do not have enough strength to raise the resistance concentrically, you still have enough strength to lower the resistance eccentrically.

TYPES

There are two main types of post-fatigue repetitions that are quite popular and productive: negatives and regressions.

Negatives

Recall that when you cannot perform the positive portion of a repetition (raise the resistance), you can still do the negative portion of a repetition (lower the resistance). This is the basis – and the value – of performing post-fatigue repetitions known as "negatives" once you can no longer raise the resistance at the end of a set. In a negative repetition, your training partner raises the resistance concentrically while you (the lifter) lower the resistance eccentrically. This is repeated for 3 - 5 repetitions with each repetition lasting about 6 - 8 seconds (depending upon the range of motion of the particular exercise).

As an example, suppose that you reached concentric muscular fatigue on a barbell bench press. Your partner would help you raise the bar off your chest until your arms are extended. Then, you lower the bar under control back to your chest. (A variation of even greater intensity is to do "forced repetitions" in which your partner adds a little extra resistance by pushing down on the bar as you lower it.) In effect, these post-fatigue repetitions are positive-assisted and negative-resisted.

Performing a few negative repetitions at the end of a set allows you to reach eccentric muscular fatigue – when your muscles have fatigued to the point that you cannot even lower the weight. And that is why a set-to-fatigue followed immediately by several negatives is so brutally effective: You have managed to exhaust your muscles completely – both concentrically and eccentrically.

Regressions

Unfortunately, one of the disadvantages of negative repetitions is that unless you have a training partner (or competent spotter), you cannot – with very few exceptions – administer them to yourself. (For the most part, you can only give yourself negatives in push-ups, dips, chins and sit-ups/crunches.)

If you do not have access to a partner, you can perform

another type of post-fatigue repetitions known as "regressions" (which are also called "breakdowns," "burnouts" and "strip sets.") When you reach concentric muscular fatigue, your muscles are still capable of producing force. However, their force-producing capacity is not enough to raise that particular level of resistance. But you could do more repetitions if you used less resistance.

When performing regressions, you (or your training partner) quickly reduce the starting resistance by about 25 - 30% and you (the lifter) do 3 - 5 regressive repetitions with the lighter load.

For instance, let us say that you just did 14 repetitions with 100 pounds on the leg extension and reached concentric muscular fatigue. You (or your training partner) would immediately decrease the resistance to about 70 - 75 pounds and would then attempt to perform 3 - 5 repetitions with the lighter load.

If you desire, you can do a second "series" of regressions. Using the previous example, you would immediately reduce the 70 - 75 pounds to about 50 - 55 pounds and try to do 3 - 5 repetitions with that resistance.

MUSCULAR FATIGUE

In order to realize your potential for increases in muscular size and strength, you must produce an appropriate level of muscular fatigue. If you create too little muscular fatigue, then you may not have stimulated gains in your muscular size and strength; if you create too much muscular fatigue, however, then you may not have stimulated gains in muscular size and strength either. Therefore, these two types of post-fatigue repetitions should be used with care.

How do you know if the stimulus is too little or too much? You should monitor your performance in the weight room in terms of resistance and repetitions. If you continue to make progress in your performance, then the stimulus is appropriate.

FIVE STEPS FOR PRODUCTIVE REPS

Regardless of the type of strength-training program that you utilize, a productive program begins with productive repetitions or "reps." Remember, the repetition is the most basic and integral aspect of a strength-training program. If your repetitions are not productive, your sets will not be productive. If your sets are not productive, your workouts will not be productive. And if your workouts are not productive, your program will not be productive. You can perform productive reps by following these five steps:

STEP #1: Raise the weight in a deliberate, controlled manner.

A repetition starts with the raising of the weight. (This is sometimes referred to as the "positive phase" of a repetition and involves a concentric muscular contraction.) You should raise the weight in a deliberate, controlled manner without any explosive or jerking movements.

Raising a weight in a rapid, explosive fashion is not recommended for two main reasons. First of all, high-velocity repetitions that are performed in a ballistic manner are actually less productive than low-velocity repetitions that are performed in a controlled manner. Here is why: When weights are lifted explosively, the muscles produce tension during the initial part of the movement . . . but not for the last part. In simple terms, the weight is practically moving by itself. In effect, the load on the muscles is decreased and so are the potential gains in muscular strength.

Unfortunately, the reduced muscular loading that occurs as a result of excessive momentum is demonstrated in weight rooms on a daily basis. As an example, have you ever seen others raise a weight so quickly on a leg-extension machine that the pad left their lower legs halfway through the repetition? Well, think about it: The pad is attached to the movement arm of the machine which, in turn, is connected to the weight by some means (such as a chain, cable or strap). If the pad is no longer in contact with the lower legs, there is no load on the muscles. If there is no load on the muscles, there is no stimulus – or reason – for them to adapt. There is no question that the more momentum is used to raise a weight, the less productive will be the repetitions.

Secondly – and more importantly – high-velocity repetitions also carry a greater risk of injury than low-velocity repetitions. Using an excessive amount of momentum to raise a weight increases the internal forces encountered by a given joint; the faster a weight is raised, the higher these forces are amplified – especially at the point of explosion. In one study, a subject squatting with 80% of his four-repetition maximum incurred a 225-pound peak shearing force during a repetition that took 4.5 seconds to complete and a 270-pound peak shearing force during a repetition that took 2.1 seconds to complete. This is clear evidence that a slower speed of movement reduces the shearing forces on joints. When the forces exceed the structural limits of a joint, an injury occurs in the muscles, connective tissues or bones. Also consider this: Dr. Fred Allman, a past president of the American College of Sports Medicine, states, "It is even possible that many injuries . . . may be the result of weakened connective tissue caused by explosive training in the weight room." In other words, explosive lifting done *inside* the weight room can predispose you to a future injury *outside* the weight room. To ensure that your repetitions are safe and productive, it should take at least 1 - 2 seconds to raise a weight.

STEP #2: Pause briefly in the position of full muscular contraction.

After raising the weight, you should pause briefly in the position of full muscular contraction or the "mid-range" position. Where is the mid-range position of a repetition? These two examples should help make it clear: When performing a leg extension, the mid-range position is where your legs are completely extended (or as straight as possible); when performing a bicep curl, the mid-range position is where your arms are completely flexed (or as bent as possible).

Most people are very weak in the mid-range position of a repetition because they rarely, if ever, emphasize it. Pausing momentarily in the mid-range position allows you to focus your attention on your muscles when they are fully contracted. Furthermore, a brief pause in the mid-range position permits a smooth transition between the raising and lowering of the weight and helps reduce the influence of momentum. If you cannot pause momentarily in the mid-range position, it is likely that you are raising the weight too quickly and throwing it into position.

STEP #3: Emphasize the lowering of the weight.

A repetition ends with the lowering of the weight. (This is sometimes referred to as the "negative phase" of a repetition and involves an eccentric muscular contraction.) The importance of emphasizing the negative phase of a repetition cannot be overstated. Numerous studies have reported that repetitions involving both concentric and eccentric contractions produce greater increases in strength than those involving just concentric contractions. Studies have also shown that optimal increases in muscular size are not obtained from weight training unless eccentric contractions are incorporated in the repetitions.

Understand that the same muscles which are used to raise a weight are also used to lower it. In a bicep curl, for example, your biceps are used in raising the weight as well as in lowering it. The only difference is that when you raise the weight, your biceps are shortening against the load and when you lower the weight, your biceps are lengthening against the load. So, by emphasizing the lowering of a weight, each repetition becomes more productive. Because a muscle lengthens as you lower a weight, emphasizing the negative phase of a repetition also ensures that the exercised muscle is being stretched properly and safely.

For any given exercise, your eccentric strength is greater than your concentric strength. From an application standpoint, this means that you can lower more weight than you can raise (again, for any given exercise). In fact, research has shown that an unfatigued muscle can lower approximately 40% more than it can raise. Stated differently, if the most weight you can raise is 100 pounds, you can probably lower about 140 pounds. Because you can lower more weight than you can raise, it stands to reason that the lowering of the weight should take more time to complete than the raising of the weight. To ensure that your repetitions are safe and productive, it should take at least 3 - 4 seconds to lower a weight back to the starting/stretched position.

In effect, it should take at least 4 - 6 seconds to perform a productive rep. Most strength coaches who are opposed to explosive, ballistic movements in the weight room consider a four- to six-second repetition to be an acceptable guideline for lifting a weight "under control" or "without an excessive amount of momentum." A 16-week study demonstrated a 50% increase in upper-body strength and a 33% increase in lower-body strength in a group that performed each repetition by raising the weight in two seconds and lowering it in four seconds. More recently, an eight-week study reported an average increase in muscular strength of 55% in 17 subjects and another eight-week study showed an average increase in muscular strength of 58.2% in 31 subjects. In both of these studies, the subjects also used the same six-second guideline for raising and lowering the weight.

STEP #4: Exercise your muscles throughout the greatest possible range of motion that safety allows.

A productive rep is done throughout the greatest possible range of motion (ROM) that safety allows – from a full stretch to a full muscular contraction and back to a full stretch. Exercising throughout a full ROM will allow you to maintain (or perhaps increase) your flexibility. Moreover, it ensures that you are stimulating your entire muscle – not just a portion of it – thereby making the repetition more productive. This point is underscored by many studies in which doing full-range repetitions were found to be a requirement for obtaining full-range effects. This does not imply that you should avoid limited-range repetitions altogether. During rehabilitation, for example, you can exercise throughout a pain-free range and still manage to stimulate some gains in muscular size and strength. Full-range repetitions are more productive, however, and should be performed whenever possible.

STEP #5: Reach concentric muscular fatigue within a prescribed range of repetitions.

The most important factor that determines your results from weight training is your inherited characteristics (which includes the insertion points of your tendons, your predominant muscle-fiber type and so on). Unfortunately, you cannot control the genetic cards that you were dealt. The most important factor that you *can* control is your level of intensity (or effort). For the most part, the harder you train, the better your response. In the weight room, a high level of intensity is characterized by exercising to the point of concentric muscular fatigue or "failure": when you have exhausted your muscles to the extent that you literally cannot raise the weight for any additional repetitions.

Failure to reach a desirable level of intensity – or muscular fatigue – will result in strength gains that are less than optimal. Evidence for this concept is found in the Overload Principle – a term that was first coined in 1933 by Dr. Arthur Steinhaus. This principle is one of the most widely referenced in exercise physiology. According to Dr. Roger Enoka – a biomechanist and author of the excellent college text *Neuromechanical Basis of Kinesiology* – the Overload Principle states, "To increase their size or functional ability, muscle fibers must be taxed toward their present capacity to respond." He adds: "This principle implies that there is a threshold point that must be exceeded before an adaptive response will occur." Stated otherwise, a minimum level of muscular fatigue must be produced in order to provide a stimulus for growth. Your intensity of effort must be great enough to exceed this threshold so that a sufficient amount of muscular fatigue is created to trigger an adaptation. Given proper nourishment and an adequate amount of recovery between workouts, your muscles will adapt to these demands by increasing in size and strength. The extent to which this "compensatory adaptation" occurs then becomes a function of your inherited characteristics.

One final point regarding muscular fatigue: Each repetition that you do is a little more productive than the previous one (as long as the number of repetitions is not excessive). In other words, the tenth repetition of your set is more productive than your ninth repetition. So, when you can no longer perform any further repetitions, the exercise is as productive as possible. Clearly, the most productive rep of a set is the last rep.

THE BOTTOM LINE

It is much safer and more productive to raise and lower the weight in a deliberate, controlled manner without any jerking or explosive movements. Raising the weight in at least 1 - 2 seconds and lowering it in at least 3 - 4 seconds ensures that momentum did not play a significant role in the performance of the repetition.

Remember, how well you lift a weight is more important than how much weight you lift. Your strength-training program will be safer and more productive when you incorporate the five steps for productive reps.

Chapter 6

ORDER OF EXERCISE

The order in which you perform your exercises is essential in producing optimal improvements in your muscular size and strength. The order of your exercises also determines which muscle(s) you emphasize or target.

PRIORITIZE!

For the most part, the idea is to exercise your most important muscles as early as possible in your workout. Clearly, it stands to reason that you would want to address those muscles while you are fresh, both mentally as well as physically.

The Neck

As a wrestler – or any other athlete who is involved in a combative sport – the most important muscles in your body are those found in your neck. The notion that your neck muscles should be your greatest priority might surprise some individuals. But think about it: It is one thing if you injure your knee, shoulder, ankle or other body part; it is an entirely different matter if you injure your neck.

At the end of your workout, you will be – and should be – physically and mentally drained. If you wait until this point to train your neck, you will be less likely to address this all-important area with a desirable level of effort or enthusiasm. So ideally, you should begin your workout with your neck exercises.

The Lower Body

Thereafter, your strength-training program should generally proceed from exercises that influence your largest muscles to those that involve your smallest muscles. Your largest and most powerful muscles are found in your lower body, specifically your hips/buttocks and legs.

What is the best order of exercise for training your lower body? Consider this: Multiple-joint movements done for your lower body – such as the leg press, deadlift and squat – require the use of your upper legs for assistance. Your upper legs – your hamstrings and quadriceps – are the "weak link" in those movements because they have a smaller amount of muscle mass. So if you fatigue your upper legs first, you will weaken an already weak link, thereby limiting the workload placed on the muscles of your hips/buttocks. Consequently, it is usually best to train your hips/buttocks before your upper legs.

What would happen if you did exercise your upper legs immediately prior to your hips/buttocks? In other words, what if you did the leg extension (for your quadriceps) and then the leg press (for your hips/buttocks)? That order of exercise would be effective in really fatiguing your quadriceps but you would not get much out of it for your hips/buttocks.

That being said, do you follow your hips/buttocks with an exercise for your hamstrings or one for your quadriceps? If you did an exercise for your hips/buttocks that also provided a significant amount of work for your hamstrings – such as a hip extension or hip-and-back movement – then you might want to train your quadriceps next so that your hamstrings get a little breather and allow them to momentarily recover; on the other hand, if you did an exercise for your hips/buttocks that also provided a great deal of work for your quadriceps – such as a leg press, deadlift or squat – then you might want to train your hamstrings next so that your quadriceps receive a slight respite and allow them to momentarily recover.

But there is another reason why you might opt to exercise your hamstrings before your quadriceps. After performing the leg extension – and assuming that you did the exercise with a high level of effort – you should notice that your quadriceps are "pumped." This is because they became engorged with blood that was redirected from other areas of your body in order to deliver oxygen to your working muscles. With such a large amount of blood pooled in your quadriceps, it might be uncomfortable for you to do the leg curl in the prone position since your "pumped" front thighs would be compressed against the pad of the machine. This would not be an issue, however, if you elected to do the leg curl in a seated position where there is no compression of the quadriceps.

After training your upper legs, you should proceed to your lower legs. If you train your calves (on the back part of your lower leg) and your dorsi flexors (on the front part of your lower leg) in the same workout, the order in which you do so really does not matter.

So in general, you should start with your hips/buttocks and literally work down your legs. In other words, the best sequence would be hips/buttocks, upper legs (hamstrings and quadriceps) and lower legs (calves or dorsi flexors).

The Torso

Once you have exercised your lower body, you can now direct your attention to your torso. What is the best order of exercise for training your torso? Not to be redundant, but from a conceptual standpoint, it sounds quite similar to that which has been discussed previously for your lower body. Multiple-joint movements done for your upper body – such as the bench press, lat pulldown and seated press – require the use of your arms to assist the movement. Your arms – your biceps, triceps and forearms – are the "weak link" in those movements because they are smaller. So if you fatigue your arms first, you will weaken an already weak link, thereby limiting the workload placed on the muscles of your torso. As a result, it is usually best to exercise your back before your biceps and your biceps before your forearms; and your chest and/or shoulders before your triceps.

What would happen if you did train your triceps immediately prior to your chest and/or shoulders or your biceps immediately prior to your upper back? In other words, what if you did the tricep extension and then the bench press or the bicep curl and then the lat pulldown? Those orders of exercise would be effective in really fatiguing your arms but you would not get much out of it for your chest or upper back.

Having said that, do you follow your torso with an exercise for your biceps or one for your triceps? If your last exercise before training your arms involved your chest and/or shoulders with assistance from your triceps – such as a bench press or seated press – then you might want to train your biceps next so that your triceps get some relief and allow them to momentarily recover; conversely, if your last exercise before training your arms involved your upper back with assistance from your biceps (and forearms) – such as a lat pulldown or seated row – then you might want to train your triceps next so that your biceps (and forearms) receive a slight respite and allow them to momentarily recover.

Here is another reason why you might want to train your biceps before your triceps: After doing a movement for your triceps – and assuming that you did it with a high level of effort – you should notice that the muscle is "pumped" (for the same reasons expressed earlier when discussing the quadriceps). With such a large amount of blood pooled in your triceps, it might not be comfortable for you to perform a bicep curl in which the backs of your arms are placed on a pad and your triceps are compressed. But this would not be a concern if you chose to perform the bicep curl in a position where there is no compression of the triceps.

You have at least two options for the order in which you exercise your chest, upper back and shoulders. One way is to do all of the exercises for a given muscle – say, your chest – and then move to the next muscle. Another way is to alternate "pushing" movements with "pulling" movements. (To avoid confusion, it is important to note that all muscles "pull" when they contract; however, muscle contractions cause joints to extend and flex which produce movements that can be described as either "pushing" or "pulling." Your chest, anterior portion of your shoulders and triceps are involved during pushing movements while your upper back, posterior portion of your shoulders and biceps are used during pulling movements.) In a "push-pull" application, you might do the following sequence for your torso: bench press (push), seated row (pull), incline press (push), lat pulldown (pull), front raise (push), bent-over raise (pull), tricep extension (push) and bicep curl (pull).

So in general, you should start with your chest, upper back and shoulders and literally work down your arms. In other words, the best order of exercise would be torso (chest, upper back and shoulders), upper arms (biceps and triceps) and lower arms (forearms).

One final note: If you prefer, you can exercise your neck musculature just after you complete your lower-body exercises – that is, prior to beginning your upper-body exercises. This will allow you to "catch your breath" between training your lower body and torso.

The Mid-Section

It is important not to fatigue your mid-section early in your workout. Your abdominals stabilize your rib cage and serve as respiratory muscles during intense exercise to facilitate forced expiration. Therefore, early fatigue of your abdominals would detract from your performance in other exercises that involve your larger, more powerful muscles.

Your lower back should be the very last muscle that you exercise. Fatiguing your lower back earlier in your workout will also hinder your performance in other movements.

So the last area that you should exercise in your workout is your mid-section. And the best order of exercise would be to train your abdominals followed by your lower back.

THE LAST REP

In summary, the best order of exercise in a total-body work-out for wrestling would usually look like this: neck, hips/buttocks, upper legs (hamstrings and quadriceps), lower legs (calves or dorsi flexors), torso (chest, upper back and shoulders), arms (biceps, triceps and forearms), abdominals and finally your lower back. If you prefer to do the so-called "split routine," this recommended order of exercise would still apply. In a workout that only targeted your chest, shoulders and triceps, for example, you should still address those body parts from largest to smallest.

Chapter 7

THE IMPORTANCE OF RECOVERY

There are three basic requirements for increasing muscular size and strength. First, your muscles must be loaded with some form of resistance that is made progressively more challenging over time. Second, your muscles must receive adequate nourishment by consuming appropriate amounts of carbohydrates, protein and fat along with sufficient quantities of vitamins and minerals. And third, your muscles must obtain enough recovery between workouts. It is the third requirement – adequate recovery – that is often ignored.

A CLOSER LOOK

Intense strength training places great demands upon your muscles. In order to adapt to those demands, your muscles must receive an ample amount of recovery between your workouts.

The "compensatory adaptation" to the demands occurs during the recovery process. Believe it or not, your muscles do not get stronger during your workout . . . your muscles get stronger *after* your workout. If the demands are of sufficient magnitude, a muscle is literally torn. Although these tears are quite small – microscopic, in fact – the recovery process is essential in that it allows the damaged muscle enough time to repair itself. Think of this as allowing a wound to heal. If you had a scab and picked at it every day, you would delay the healing process. But if you left it alone, you would permit the damaged tissue time to heal. So in a sense, the recovery following a workout is a process in which damaged tissue – in this case, muscle tissue – is healed.

There are individual variations in recovery ability – everyone has different levels of tolerance for exercise. However, a period of at least 48 hours is usually necessary for muscle tissue to recover sufficiently from an intense workout in the weight room. Keep in mind, too, that intense strength training relies heavily upon carbohydrates as the primary source of energy. Adequate recovery is required to return the carbohydrate (or glycogen) stores to their pre-training levels. It appears as if about 48 hours are also needed to replenish the carbohydrate stores that are depleted as a result of intense physical exertion. As such, it is suggested that you perform your strength training 2 - 3 times per week on nonconsecutive days (such as on Monday, Wednesday and Friday). This advice is consistent with the recommendation of the American College of Sports Medicine. (Note that this assumes total-body workouts.) Can you achieve significant improvements in strength by doing just two weekly workouts? Absolutely. In one study that involved 117 subjects, a group that trained two times per week experienced approximately 80% of the gains in strength of the group that trained three times per week.

An appropriate frequency (and volume) of strength training can be likened to doses of medication. In order for medicine to improve a condition, it must be taken at specific intervals and in certain amounts. Taking medicine at a greater frequency or in a larger quantity beyond what is needed can have harmful effects. Similarly, an "overdose" of strength training – in which workouts are done too often or have too much volume – can also be detrimental.

Most individuals respond well from three total-body workouts per week. But because of a low tolerance for strength training, others respond more favorably from two total-body workouts per week. (In rare circumstances, an individual may respond better from one total-body workout per week.) Performing any more than three "doses" of total-body workouts per week will gradually become counterproductive if the demands placed upon your muscles exceed your recovery ability.

IN-SEASON STRENGTH TRAINING

Most authorities have suggested that a muscle begins to lose strength (and size) if it is not adequately stimulated within 48 - 96 hours of a previous workout. Some anecdotal reports suggest that it may be more than this time frame – at least for some individuals. Clearly, however, a loss of muscular strength (and size) will occur after some period of extended inactivity. As an athlete, then, it is important for you to continue strength training even while in-season or while competing. However, you should reduce the number of your workouts to twice a week due to the increased activity level of practices and meets/ matches. One workout should be done as soon as possible following a match but not within 48 hours of your next match. So if you wrestle on Saturday and Tuesday, you should do your strength training on Sunday and Wednesday (or Thursday, provided that you have at least 48 hours before your next competition). From time to time, you may only be able to do strength training once per week because of a particularly heavy schedule such as wrestling three times in one week or several days in a row at a tournament.

How do you know if your muscles have had an adequate amount of recovery? You should see a gradual improvement in the amount of resistance and/or number of repetitions that you are able to do over the course of several weeks. If not, then you are probably not getting enough recovery between your workouts – which could be the result of performing too many sets, too many repetitions or too many exercises. Remember, strength training will be effective if it provides an *overload* not an *overdose*.

THE SPLIT ROUTINE

A method that has been popularized by bodybuilders and competitive weightlifters is known as the "split routine." When using a split routine, the body is divided – or "split" – into different parts that are trained on different days. There are many possibilities for a split routine. One example would be to split the muscles such that the hips, legs and mid-section are trained on Monday and Thursday; the chest, shoulders and triceps on Tuesday and Friday; and the upper back, biceps and forearms on Wednesday and Saturday. So in this split routine, each muscle would be trained twice per week during six workouts.

Despite the popularity of split routines, they are no more effective than total-body workouts. In a study involving 30 subjects, one group did a split routine consisting of four workouts per week (two for the upper body and two for the lower body) and another group did two total-body workouts per week. (A third group served as the control and did not train.) After 20 weeks of training, the researchers concluded that both protocols were equally effective in improving maximum strength, increasing lean-body mass and decreasing body fat.

Split routines can be productive as long as they encourage progressive overload and provide adequate recovery. It is the latter area in which split routines often fall short. If a split routine is designed correctly, an individual will not train the same muscles two days in a row. Recall, however, that it takes about 48 hours for your body to replenish its stockpiles of carbohydrates following an intense workout. (Again, carbohydrates are the principal fuel during intense exercise.) So if you trained your lower body on Monday with a desirable level of intensity, you exhausted much of your carbohydrate stores. Even if you train different muscles on Tuesday, your body may not have had enough time to fully recover those carbohydrate stores. Keep in mind, too, that even though you may train part of your body in a workout, you still stress your entire anaerobic energy pathways (which provide metabolic support for your efforts in the weight room). Your energy systems do not recover in parts – they recover as a whole. The researchers in the aforementioned study that compared split routines to total-body workouts noted that doing fewer workouts per week in the weight room "would free more days for recovery or other types of training." This is an important consideration for wrestlers who must invest significant amounts of time in aerobic and anaerobic conditioning and skill development.

If you prefer to use a split routine, make sure that you group your muscles based upon their functions and relations with other muscles. For instance, your triceps and shoulders are used to train your chest and your biceps and forearms are used to train your upper back. As such, muscles with common functions should be trained together.

One final point: From a performance perspective, split routines do not make sense because they are not specific to the muscular involvement in wrestling. When you use a split routine, you train different muscles on different days. However, a selective use of muscles almost never happens during a wrestling match. Rather, you are required to integrate all of your muscles at once. Therefore, it makes little sense for you to prepare for wrestling by training your muscles separately on different days.

THE LAST REP

While there are certainly other important ingredients in a strength-training program, the basic requirements are progressive overload, proper nutrition and adequate recovery. So if you want a muscle to get larger and stronger, you must stress it, feed it and rest it!

Chapter 8
DOCUMENTING YOUR PERFORMANCE IN THE WEIGHT ROOM

Many athletes believe that they do not need to use a workout card because they can remember their resistance and repetitions. In all likelihood, they have probably been lifting the same resistance and doing the same repetitions for so long that the numbers have become firmly entrenched in their long-term memories. The fact of the matter is that it is absolutely critical to keep written records that are accurate and detailed if strength training is to be as productive as possible.

Why? For one thing, records document the history of what you accomplished during each and every exercise of each and every strength session. Moreover, maintaining records is an extremely valuable tool to monitor your progress and make your workouts more meaningful. Records can also be used to identify exercises in which you have reached a plateau. In the unfortunate event of an injury, you can also gauge the effectiveness of your rehabilitative training if you have a record of your pre-injury levels of strength.

A workout card can have an infinite number of appearances and need not be elaborate. However, you should be able to record your bodyweight, the date of each workout, the resistance used for each exercise, the number of repetitions performed for each exercise, the order in which the exercises were completed and any necessary seat adjustments.

Some of the more common exercises can be listed on the workout card (such as the leg extension, bench press and bicep curl). Or, the workout card can contain blank spaces so that you can fill in your own menu of exercises. The recommended repetition ranges should also be given for each exercise.

RECORDING DATA

Perhaps the best way to illustrate the correct way for you to record your data on a workout card – as well as to understand the application of the Double-Progressive Technique – is to detail several imaginary workouts. In the upcoming discussion, please refer to Figure 8.1 where data from four workouts (using single-set training) have been recorded for the period of September 22 - 29. Due to space constraints, the data for our fictional athlete – named Ryan Rassler – have been limited to details of the first eight exercises in his total-body workout.

September 22: Ryan started his workout by performing lateral neck flexion (to the right and left). He was able to do 11 repetitions with 105 pounds in both exercises. After training his neck, he performed the leg press as his hip exercise. Note that he used 275 pounds and managed 18 repetitions. He then did 15 repetitions on the prone leg curl with 100 pounds. Using 160 pounds on the leg extension, he performed 10 repetitions. Ryan's third and final leg exercise (his sixth overall) was the seated calf raise. In this movement, he did 17 repetitions with 120 pounds. In the bench press, he managed 8 repetitions with 180 pounds. As a second chest exercise (his eighth overall), the athlete chose the bent-arm fly. Here, he performed 8 repetitions with a pair of 40-pound dumbbells.

September 24: Two days later during his second workout of the week, Ryan again began with his neck exercises. This time, however, he elected to perform two different exercises: neck flexion and neck extension (using manual resistance or "MR"). After completing these two exercises, the athlete moved to the leg press. Because he was not able to do the maximal number of repetitions during his previous workout, note that he used the same resistance. On this date, however, he performed 20 repetitions with 275 pounds – an improvement of two repetitions. In his previous workout, he was able to do the maximal number of repetitions on the prone leg curl, so he increased the resistance by 2.5 pounds – from 100 to 102.5. The athlete managed 14 repetitions with the new resistance. During the leg extension, he again used 160 pounds but was able to do 11 repetitions – one more than the last time. Since

Ryan exceeded the maximal number of repetitions on the seated calf raise in his previous workout, he increased the resistance from 120 to 122.5 pounds and did 16 repetitions with it. In the bench press, he repeated 180 pounds and managed 9 repetitions – an improvement of one repetition compared to his preceding workout. During the bent-arm fly, the athlete again used 40-pound dumbbells and improved his repetitions from 8 to 9.

September 26: Ryan started off his third and final workout of the week by doing lateral neck flexion (again to the right and left). Since he did not do the maximal number of repetitions the last time that he performed those two exercises, he used the same resistance but was able to do 12 repetitions. His next exercise was the leg press in which he increased the resistance by 5 pounds – from 275 to 280 – and did 19 repetitions. For the second consecutive workout, the athlete managed 14 repetitions with 102.5 pounds on the prone leg curl. On the leg extension, he used the same resistance as the previous workout – 160 pounds – but was able to do one more repetition. He increased the resistance on the seated calf raise from 122.5 to 125 pounds and performed 15 repetitions. The athlete again used 180 pounds on the bench press and was able to perform 10 repetitions – one more than his previous workout. In the bent-arm fly, he used 40-pound dumbbells again and did the same number of repetitions as the last time.

September 29: During his first workout of the second week, Ryan began his workout with neck flexion and neck extension (using manual resistance). On this date, he decided to change his hip exercise from the leg press to the deadlift (with a trap bar) and was able to do 20 repetitions with 205 pounds. Next, he moved to the prone leg curl and performed 15 repetitions with 102.5 pounds – an improvement of one repetition compared to his previous workout. Using 160 pounds on the leg extension, he again did 12 repetitions. Ryan completed his lower-body exercises by doing 14 repetitions on the seated calf raise with an increased resistance of 127.5 pounds. In the bench press, he again did 10 repetitions with 180 pounds. And in the bent-arm fly, he performed 10 repetitions – one more than in his last workout – with the 40-pound dumbbells.

October 1: The resistance for each exercise has been recorded for this workout based upon Ryan's performance in his prior workout. Note that the resistance was increased on lateral neck flexion (right and left) as well as the deadlift and prone leg curl because he performed the maximal number of repetitions during his previous workout. The resistance remained the same on the leg extension, bench press and bent-arm fly. Finally, the athlete chose to perform dorsi flexion (with manual resistance) as his lower-leg exercise instead of the seated calf raise.

The bottom line: Do not underestimate the importance of using a workout card in making your strength training more productive and more meaningful.

NAME: Ryan Rassler				DATE:	Mon 09-22	Wed 09-24	Fri 09-26	Mon 09-29	Wed 10-01
				BW:	162	162	161	162	
	EXERCISE	REPS	SEAT		wt/reps	wt/reps	wt/reps	wt/reps	wt/reps
Neck (2-4)	Neck Lateral Flexion/R	8-12	5		105/11		105/12		107.5
	Neck Lateral Flexion/L	8-12	5		105/11		105/12		107.5
	Neck Flexion	8-12	5			MR/12		MR/12	
	Neck Extension	8-12	5			MR/12		MR/12	
Hips (1)	Leg Press	15-20	7½		275/18	275/20	280/19		
	Deadlift	15-20						205/20	207.5
Upper Legs (2)	Prone Leg Curl	10-15			100/15	102.5/14	102.5/14	102.5/15	105
	Leg Extension	10-15	3½		160/10	160/11	160/12	160/12	160
Lower Legs (1)	Seated Calf Raise	10-15			120/17	122.5/16	125/15	127.5/14	
	Dorsi Flexion	10-15							MR
Chest (2)	Bench Press	6-12			180/8	180/9	180/10	180/10	180
	Bent-Arm Fly	6-12			40/8	40/9	40/9	40/10	40

FIGURE 8.1: RECORDING WORKOUT DATA (SINGLE-SET TRAINING)

Chapter 9

IMPROVING POWER FOR WRESTLING

One of the most important aspects of performance potential is power. It is no surprise, then, that coaches and wrestlers are constantly looking for ways to improve this valuable physical quality.

It has long been thought that you must perform the so-called "quick lifts" – such as the power clean, push press, snatch and/or their derivatives – and do fast-speed repetitions to improve power. When coaches or wrestlers learn that our wrestling staff does not advocate these methods, they sometimes comment that we don't "train for power" or do "power training." The fact of the matter is that our wrestlers "train for power" and do "power training" – but not by implementing the quick lifts or fast-speed repetitions.

How is it possible for wrestlers (or other athletes) to improve their power without using these methods?

WHAT IS POWER?

Before discussing how power can be improved, it is important to understand the meaning of the term. In physics, a mathematical definition of "power" is "work divided by time." Since "work" is defined as "force times distance," it follows that power is also "force times distance divided by time."

Another definition of "power" is "force times velocity." The term "velocity" is defined as "distance divided by time." Once again, it follows that "power" is "force times distance divided by time."

So power has three variables: force, distance and time. Manipulating any of these three variables will affect power.

METHODS FOR IMPROVEMENT

Based upon the equation "power equals force times distance divided by time," you can improve power output three different ways: (1) increase the amount of force; (2) increase the distance of application; and (3) decrease the time of application.

Increase the Amount of Force

If you increase the amount of force that you apply and keep the other two variables in the equation the same – namely, the distance over which you apply the force and the time that it takes you to apply the force – you will produce more power. Here is an example: If you can bench press 160 pounds a distance of 18 inches (1.5 feet) in 2 seconds, your power output is 120 foot-pounds per second. [160 lbs x 1.5 ft ÷ 2 sec = 120 ft-lbs/sec.] Suppose that at some point in the future, you increased your bench press to 180 pounds. Assuming that the distance you moved the resistance (18 inches) and the time it took you to move the resistance (2 seconds) remained the same, your power output is now 135 foot-pounds per second. So by increasing the amount of force that you applied, you have improved your power output.

How do you increase the amount of force that you apply? The short answer is to increase the strength of your muscles. If you increase the strength of your muscles, they can produce more force; if your muscles produce more force, you will have the potential to produce more power.

How do you improve your strength so that you can produce more force? While there is no shortage of opinions, any strength-training program will be productive if – and only if – it incorporates the Overload Principle. Arguably, this principle is the most important underlying construct for improving physical performance – whether it is strength, endurance or even flexibility. As far as strength training is concerned, the principle suggests that in order for a muscle to increase in strength it must be stressed – or "overloaded" – with a workload that is beyond its present capacity.

You can overload your muscles by using the Double-Progressive Technique. When implementing this technique, over-load is accomplished by two means. One way is to make the resistance – or the "load" – progressively more challenging over time; another way is to do more repetitions with the same resistance. A muscle will adapt to the "overload" – from using a heavier amount of resistance or performing a greater number of repetitions – by increasing in strength. Without imposing greater demands, there will not be any compensatory adaptation because a muscle will literally have no reason to get stronger. Stated otherwise, a muscle must be exposed to demands that it has not experienced previously.

Also remember that it matters little whether a muscle is loaded with resistance from machines, barbells, dumbbells, stretch cords, sandbags, bricks or even other human beings. A muscle does not possess the ability to distinguish between different modes of resistance. It simply responds to being loaded.

Increase the Distance of Application

If you increase the distance over which you apply the force and do not change the other two variables in the equation – specifically, the amount of force that you apply and the time that it takes you to apply the force – you will produce more power. Consider this example: If you can squat 300 pounds a distance of 21 inches (1.75 feet) in 2 seconds, your power output is 262.5 foot-pounds per second. [300 lbs x 1.75 ft ÷ 2 sec = 262.5 ft-lbs/sec.] Suppose that at some point in the future, you increased your range of motion in the squat so that you are now displacing the resistance a distance of 24 inches. Assuming that the resistance you lifted (300 pounds) and the time it took you to move the resistance (2 seconds) did not change, your power output is now 300 foot-pounds per second. So by increasing the distance over which you applied the force, you have improved your power output.

How do you increase the distance over which you apply force? One way is to become more flexible. If you become more flexible, you can increase the ranges of motion of your joints; if you increase the ranges of motion of your joints, you will have the potential to produce more power.

How do you improve your flexibility so that you can apply force over a greater distance? Like strength training, there is no one optimal program for improving flexibility. Successful flexibility programs, however, have several commonalities. To reduce your risk of injury, you should stretch under control without any bouncing, bobbing or jerking movements. Moreover, you should hold the stretched position for about 30 - 60 seconds. Similar to strength training, you must make your flexibility training progressively more challenging. You can do this by attempting to stretch a little bit farther than the last time. Finally, it is important to stretch each of your major muscle groups and do so on a regular basis.

Decrease the Time of Application

If you decrease the time that it takes you to apply the force and keep the other two variables in the equation the same – namely the amount of force that you apply and the distance over which you apply the force – you will produce more power. Here is an example: If you can deadlift 400 pounds a distance of 18 inches (1.5 feet) in 2 seconds, your power output is 300 foot-pounds per second. [400 lbs x 1.5 ft ÷ 2 sec = 300 ft-lbs/ sec.] Suppose that at some point in the future, you increased your speed of movement in the deadlift to 1.5 seconds (that is, you did the repetition faster). Assuming that the resistance you lifted (400 pounds) and the distance you moved the resistance (18 inches) remained constant, your power output is now 400 foot-pounds per second. So by increasing the speed at which you applied force, you have improved your power output.

How do you decrease the time that it takes you to apply force? One alternative is to perfect your wrestling technique. If you perfect your technique, you can perform the skill more quickly; if you can perform the skill more quickly, you will have the potential to produce more power.

How do you improve your technique so that you can decrease the time that it takes you to apply force? The motor-learning literature is in general agreement as to how this can be best achieved. It is important that you learn how to do the skill correctly. In addition, you must perform the skill over and over again until you can execute it without conscious effort. The skill must be practiced in a flawless manner. Remember, practice makes perfect . . . but only if you practice perfect.

Lastly, the skill should be practiced exactly as you would use it on the wrestling mat. Tim Wakeham, Assistant Strength and Conditioning Coach at Michigan State University, offers this insight: "Students do not study algebra to take a geometry test even though those are similar subjects. Both subjects are under the umbrella of mathematics, and because of their similarities, studying one may positively affect test results in the other. But it should be obvious that the *best* results would come from preparing for an algebra test by studying algebra."

MAT APPLICATIONS

Examples in the weight room were given to illustrate how the three variables in the power equation – that is, force, distance and time – can be manipulated to improve power output. Several applications of those concepts can also be illustrated on the wrestling mat:

- If you apply more force over the same distance in the same amount of time, you will have the potential to lift an opponent with more power.
- If you move a greater distance (without overpenetrating) with the same amount of force in the same amount of time, you will have the potential to execute a double-leg takedown with more power.
- If you move in less time with the same amount of force over the same distance, you will have the potential to perform a fireman's carry with more power.

POWER TO YOU!

So an athlete who is powerful can apply a large force over a long distance in a short period of time. As demonstrated earlier, your power output can be improved by three different means: (1) increase the amount of force that you apply; (2) increase the distance over which you apply the force; and (3) decrease the amount of time that it takes you to apply the force. This can be accomplished by improving your strength, flexibility and technique.

Be forewarned, however, that just because you can produce more power during a given exercise in the weight room does not mean that you will automatically produce more power during a given skill on the wrestling mat. Simply stated, there is no legitimate, scientific evidence that the ability to produce power transfers from one activity to another.

Think about it: If doing power cleans or another explosive-type movement improves your stand up, for example, then doing stand ups should improve your power clean. But they do not. The bottom line is that producing power in the weight room is one thing and producing power on the wrestling mat is another.

Chapter 10

BACK WITH A VENGEANCE

Quite often, individuals tend to overemphasize the muscles that they can see and underemphasize – or even overlook – muscles that they cannot. For instance, the chest on the anterior part of the body usually receives a good bit of attention – in many cases, far too much – while the upper back on the posterior part of the body typically does not get equal emphasis. Yet, the muscles of the upper back are at least as important as those of the chest.

BASIC ANATOMY AND MUSCULAR FUNCTION

The latissimus dorsi is the long, broad muscle that comprises most of your upper back. The "lats" are the largest muscles in your upper body. Their primary function is to pull your upper arm backward and downward. The lats are especially important in pulling movements that are done on the wrestling mat and in the weight room. In addition, developing the lats is necessary to provide muscular balance between your upper-back and chest areas.

Regardless of hand positioning, just about any type of pulling movement for the torso – whether it be rowing, chinning or any pulldown variation – targets the same muscles, namely your upper back, biceps and forearms. However, there are differences in the leverage received from these muscles based upon the grip that you elect to use. For example, performing a lat pulldown with an underhand grip (palms facing toward you) is more biomechanically efficient than doing it with an overhand grip (palms facing away from you). Why? With an underhand grip, the radius and ulna (your forearm bones) run parallel to one another; with an overhand grip, the radius crosses over the ulna forming an "X". In this position, the bicep tendon gets wrapped around the lower portion of the radius, creating a biomechanical disadvantage and a loss in leverage. This is also true when comparing an underhand and overhand grip during rowing and chinning movements – the same muscles are used but with varying degrees of biomechanical leverage. (With a "parallel grip" – in which your palms face each other – your forearm bones do not cross, either. Therefore, this grip is also more efficient than an overhand one.)

What grip should you use? While there is a biomechanical advantage in using an underhand (and parallel) grip, movements done with an overhand grip can still be productive. Therefore, the grip that you use is your choice.

GENERAL GUIDELINES AND PRECAUTIONS

The following general guidelines apply when training your upper-back musculature:

1. Do exercises for your upper back prior to those for your biceps and forearms. Here is why: Multiple-joint movements require the use of smaller, weaker muscles to assist in the exercise. (As a rule of thumb, your legs are the weak link when performing multiple-joint movements for your hips and your arms are the weak link when performing multiple-joint movements for your upper body.) If you fatigue your smaller muscles first – in this case, your biceps and forearms – you will weaken an already weak link. As a result, you will limit the workload placed on the larger, more powerful muscles of your upper-back region and restrict the potential for their development.

2. Provide equal attention to the muscles of your upper back and chest. These muscles – as well as all others in your body – are arranged in such a way that they perform opposing functions: Your upper back moves your upper arm in one direction and your chest moves your upper arm in the opposite direction. When one muscle acts in opposition to another, it is referred to as an "an-

tagonist." It is important to provide antagonistic partnerships with an equal – or nearly equal – amount of stimulus so that a muscular imbalance does not occur between the two areas. In this regard, strong upper-back muscles are necessary to balance the effects of the chest muscles. Therefore, you should perform approximately the same volume of activity – that is, roughly the same number of exercises, sets and repetitions – for your upper back as you do for your chest.

3. Avoid doing exercises in which you experience shoulder pain. Some individuals may find it difficult – or even impossible – to perform pain-free exercises when they pull the bar behind their heads such as during the lat pulldown or pull-up. In fact, this position may exacerbate shoulder-impingement syndrome. Simply doing those same two exercises with the bar positioned in front of your head – rather than behind it – will reduce the orthopedic stress in your shoulder area. This is not to say that pulling the bar behind your head cannot be done. Rather, pulling the bar behind your head should not be performed if it cannot be done in a pain-free manner.

4. Perform your repetitions with proper technique. Proper technique is raising the resistance without an excessive use of momentum in about 1 - 2 seconds, pausing distinctly in the mid-range (or contracted) position and lowering the resistance under control in about 3 - 4 seconds. This will ensure that momentum did not play a significant role in the performance of the repetition and that your chances of incurring an injury while strength training are minimized. In addition, each repetition should be done throughout a full range of motion (ROM). This will allow you to maintain (or perhaps improve) your flexibility and guarantee that you are exercising your entire muscle, not just a portion of it.

5. Reach muscular fatigue within about 6 - 12 repetitions (or about 40 - 70 seconds). A desirable level of fatigue is when you have exhausted your muscles to the point

where you literally cannot do another repetition. Performing sets of less than about 6 repetitions increases your risk of injury. Once an activity for the upper back exceeds about 12 repetitions, it becomes an increasingly greater test of aerobic endurance rather than muscular strength.

6. Train the muscles of your upper back 2 - 3 times per week on nonconsecutive days. You should exercise your upper-back muscles three times per week when not in season and twice per week when in season (but not within 48 hours of a match).

EXERCISES AND DESCRIPTIONS

The following are specific descriptions for many popular exercises that can be performed to strengthen the muscles of your upper back using conventional equipment:

Bent-Over Row

This multiple-joint movement works your upper back, biceps and forearms. Place your left hand and left knee on a bench and position your right foot on the floor at a comfortable distance from the bench. Reach down with your right hand and grasp a dumbbell. Lift the dumbbell slightly off the floor and keep your right arm straight. Your right palm should be facing the bench. To do the exercise, keep your upper arm close to your torso and pull the dumbbell to your right shoulder. Pause briefly in this mid-range position (arm flexed) and then return the dumbbell under control to the starting position (arm fully extended) to ensure an adequate stretch. After performing a set for the right side of your body, repeat the exercise for the left side of your body (with your right hand and right knee on the bench for support).

Seated Row (with chest pad)

Your upper back, biceps and forearms are targeted with this multiple-joint movement. If the seat pad on the machine is adjustable, position it so that when you pull the handles toward you, your hands will be just below your shoulders. If the chest pad is adjustable, position it so that you can barely touch the handles with your fingertips. Grasp the handles and lean toward the chest pad. To do the movement, keep your upper arms close to your torso and pull the handles directly below your shoulders. Pause briefly in this mid-range position (arms flexed) and then lower the weight under control to the starting position (arms fully extended) to obtain an adequate stretch.

Seated Row (without chest pad)

This multiple-joint movement exercises your upper back, biceps and forearms. Grasp the handles and lean back slightly. To do the movement, keep your upper arms close to your torso and pull the handles to your mid-section. Pause briefly in this mid-range position (arms flexed) and then lower the weight under control to the starting position (arms fully extended) to ensure a sufficient stretch.

Underhand Lat Pulldown

Your upper back, biceps and forearms will be targeted with this multiple-joint movement. Grasp the bar with your palms facing toward your body and space your hands approximately shoulder-width apart. Sit down on the seat pad, place your upper thighs under the roller pads and lean back slightly. To do the movement, pull the bar to your upper chest and bring your elbows past your torso. Pause briefly in this mid-range position (arms flexed) and then return the weight under control to the starting position (arms fully extended) to obtain a proper stretch.

Overhand Lat Pulldown

This multiple-joint movement works your upper back, biceps and forearms. Grasp the bar with your palms facing away from your body and space your hands several inches wider than shoulder-width apart. (You should not use an excessively wide grip since this will reduce your ROM.) Sit down on the seat pad and place your upper thighs under the roller pads. To do the exercise, pull the bar behind your head to the base of your neck. Pause briefly in this mid-range position (arms flexed) and then lower the weight under control to the starting position (arms fully extended) to ensure an adequate stretch. This exercise may be contraindicated if you have shoulder-impingement syndrome. You may be able to do this exercise in a pain-free manner, however, by pulling the bar in front of your head (to the upper part of your chest) rather than behind it.

Chin

Your upper back, biceps and forearms will be addressed with this multiple-joint movement. Reach up, grasp the bar with your palms facing toward your body and space your hands approximately shoulder-width apart. Bring your body to a "dead hang" and cross your ankles. To do the movement, pull yourself upward, touch your upper chest to the bar and bring your elbows past your torso. Pause briefly in this mid-range position (arms flexed) and then lower your body under control to the starting position (arms fully extended) to obtain a proper stretch.

Pull-Up

This multiple-joint movement works your upper back, biceps and forearms. Reach up, grasp the bar with your palms facing away from your body and space your hands several inches wider than shoulder-width apart. (You should not use an excessively wide grip since this will reduce your ROM.) Bring your body to a "dead hang" and cross your ankles. To do the movement, pull yourself upward and touch the base of your neck to the bar. Pause briefly in this mid-range position (arms flexed) and then lower your body under control to the starting position (arms fully extended) to ensure a sufficient stretch. This exercise may be contraindicated if you have shoulder-impingement syndrome. However, you may be able to do this exercise in a pain-free manner by pulling the bar in front of your head (to the upper part of your chest) rather than behind it.

Pullover (machine)

This single-joint movement targets your upper back without using your biceps and forearms. Adjust the seat pad so that your shoulders are slightly below the axis of rotation when sitting upright with your arms hanging straight down. Secure the seat belt, place your torso against the back pad and put your feet on the foot bar. Push the foot bar forward with your legs and place the backs of your upper arms against the elbow pads. Position your hands on the movement arm so that your palms are facing the bar and your hands are open – that is, your fingers are extended. (If you cannot reach the bar while keeping your elbows against the pads, you can grasp it with an underhand grip.) Remove your feet from the foot bar and position the movement arm near or slightly behind your head. To do the exercise, pull the movement arm down to your mid-section by exerting force against the elbow pads (or by pulling the bar with your hands if you have grabbed it). Pause briefly in this mid-range position (hands near your mid-section) and then lower the weight under control to the starting position (elbows near or slightly past your head) to ensure a sufficient stretch. After completing the exercise, place your feet back on the foot bar, remove your arms from the machine and use your legs to return the resistance to the rest of the weight stack. This exercise may be contraindicated for individuals with low-back pain or shoulder impingement syndrome.

Pullover (dumbbell/barbell)

You can exercise your upper back without using your biceps and forearms with this single-joint movement. Lay supine across the width of a bench (not the length) and position the weight (a barbell or dumbbell) over your chest at arms length (or have a spotter give you the weight). To do the movement, keep your arms relatively straight, lower the weight under control to the stretched position (elbows near or slightly past your head) and then pull the weight back to the starting position (which, in this case, is the mid-range position). This exercise may be contraindicated for individuals with low-back pain or shoulder-impingement syndrome.

A powerful grip is a sign of a powerful individual. On the wrestling mat, your grip strength is extremely critical in controlling your opponent; in the weight room, your grip strength is also important since it is used in many multiple-joint movements that target your torso. Remember, too, that grip strength is not limited to athletic endeavors – an abundance of everyday activities also involve gripping.

So the importance of having a strong grip is well established. Of the muscles that are involved directly with gripping, the ones that receive the least amount of attention are those that flex your fingers. Also consider this: A study in the February 2002 issue of *Biomechanics* determined that the four fingers do not produce equal amounts of gripping force. This information, in itself, is really no great surprise to the wrestling community. But what is of interest is that the study quantified the force production of the four fingers. It was found that the force-sharing percentages of your fingers (at an optimal angle of your wrist) are as follows: index 32.2%, middle 32.6%, ring 23.5% and little 11.7%. So of the total force in gripping, roughly one third is produced by the index finger, one third by the middle finger and one third by the collective efforts of the ring and little fingers. The implication of this information is that you should address the two fingers that contribute the least amount of gripping force – namely your ring and little fingers – to strengthen the weak link.

EXERCISES

Needless to say, relatively few people do any direct work for their finger flexors . . . and even less do any direct work to isolate their ring and little fingers. Yet, the importance of strengthening these muscles cannot be overstated. Therefore, it is a good idea to target these muscles on a regular basis.

While it is difficult to provide direct work for the ring and little fingers, it is not impossible. One effective exercise that can be slightly modified to isolate and strengthen these two fingers is finger flexion. You can do this movement by utilizing a low pulley with a short bar attached to a cable. Simply stand up, keep your arms straight and grasp the ends of the bar with your palms facing away from you using only your ring and little fingers. To do the exercise, pull the bar to the mid-range position (fingers flexed) without using your arms or other body parts – just your ring and little fingers. Pause briefly in this position – while squeezing the bar as hard as possible – and then lower the bar under control to the starting position (fingers extended) at the end of each repetition to provide an adequate stretch. Attempt to lower the bar all the way down to your fingertips – to the point where the bar almost drops from your two fingers. Do not throw the weight by using your legs or by swinging your torso back and forth – movement should only occur around your finger joints. Besides using a low pulley with a short bar attachment, you can also do this exercise in a similar fashion using manual resistance.

ACTIVITIES

You can also perform a few activities to strengthen your ring and little fingers. An excellent activity is to squeeze a ball using just these two fingers. This activity has its shortcomings in that the resistance is somewhat limited. Nevertheless, it makes for a great way to isolate your ring and little fingers. Using only these two fingers, you can either squeeze a rubber ball as hard as possible for 60 seconds or do 60 seconds worth of slow, deliberate repetitions. Either way, the idea is to isolate your ring and little fingers.

Another activity that can be used to improve the strength of your ring and little fingers is to pop bubble wrap. This unusual activity involves the use of bubble wrap that is often found in shipping packages. Simply take a section of the bubble wrap and pop each of the bubbles by pressing the tips of your ring and little fingers to your palms. Do not press with your thumbs or other fingers – just your ring and little fingers.

GET A GRIP!

By doing direct work for the muscles that affect your fingers, you will increase your grip strength. Clearly, improving the strength of your gripping muscles can turn a weak link into a strong suit.

Chapter 12

WHICH ARE BETTER:
FREE WEIGHTS OR MACHINES?

The two most popular types of equipment that are used for weight training are free weights (barbells and dumbbells) and machines (either selectorized or plate-loaded). Accompanying their popularity is a fiery and emotional debate that has raged for decades over which of the two modalities is better for weight training.

ISSUES AND ANSWERS

Why the squabble? Much of the debate centers on two major issues: muscular response and athletic specificity.

Muscular Response

How many times have you heard that free weights are more advantageous for building muscular size and strength whereas machines are merely for toning and shaping muscles? Is this a reasonable assertion?

In order to examine this matter, it is first necessary to understand the requirements for increasing the size and strength of muscles. Stimulating these desired myological improvements is not really all that complicated. First of all, a resistance (or "load") must be applied to a muscle. Second, the resistance must be made progressively more challenging from one workout to the next. It is that simple. Certainly, other ingredients are also important in a weight-training program. But in order for you to improve your muscular size and strength, the two most basic requirements are that your muscles must first be loaded with a resistance and then progressively overloaded.

What about the nature of the resistance? A number of studies have shown that you will not develop one way with free weights and another way with machines. One 10-week study compared two groups who trained three times per week with either free weights or machines. Both groups significantly increased their strength and lean-body mass and deceased their body fat. Moreover, there were no significant differences between the two groups. In another 10-week study, the researchers found no significant differences in strength increases between a group who used machines and a group who used free weights.

The bottom line is that your muscles cannot possibly "know" whether the source of the resistance is a barbell, a dumbbell, a selectorized machine, a plate-loaded machine or a cinder block. The sole factors in determining your muscular response from weight training are your genetic makeup and your level of intensity – not the equipment that you used.

Athletic Specificity

The second area of controversy generally pertains to the concept of specificity. In this regard, some individuals feel that specific sports skills can be improved by simulating them with added resistance. Unfortunately, the motor-learning literature does not seem to support this assertion. In one study, competitive swimmers were filmed while sprinting the butterfly. The films were digitized and analyzed by computer. Among other things, it was found that swimming with added resistance was done with noticeably different – and less effective – stroke mechanics compared to swimming without added resistance. In effect, the swimmers were performing a totally different skill.

The same result occurs when attempting to mimic the movement pattern of a particular sports skill in the weight room with a barbell or a dumbbell. The fact of the matter is that no exercise done in the weight room – with a barbell, dumbbell or machine – will help you to improve your wrestling skills. At best, this is a waste of time and energy.

Another related argument is that balancing a barbell or a dumbbell is advantageous because this balance will transfer or "carry over" to sports skills. Once again, the relevant research does not appear to confirm this claim. In one study, researchers examined six tests of dynamic and static balance and found that the abilities supporting one test of balance were separate from those supporting another. In other words, the ability to balance a barbell is quite different from the ability to maintain your balance on the mat. Adds John Thomas, the Strength and Conditioning Coach at Penn State (for football), "[Using] free weights may develop general balance but not specific sport skills."

The next time that you watch other wrestlers, see if you can tell which ones use free weights, which ones use machines, which ones use a combination and which ones use no type of weight training whatsoever. Obviously, it would be impossible to tell because the source of resistance matters very little, if any, in an athlete's response to weight training.

PROS AND CONS

That said, there are a number of pros and cons to both free weights and machines which may have an impact upon your choice of equipment.

Advantages of Free Weights

Free weights have the following advantages over machines:

1. If you are a coach who is trying to outfit a weight room with a limited or tight budget, the most important consideration in your choice of equipment may very well be the cost. Machines are generally much more expensive than free weights. You could easily pay more than $40,000 for a complete "line" of state-of-the-art selectorized equipment (10 - 12 machines). That same number of plate-loaded machines would be much less expensive but remember a possible "hidden" cost: You may need to purchase a few thousand pounds of plates to serve as the resistance for the machines. A considerable amount of free-weight equipment could be purchased for much less of an investment.

2. Most machines that are geared toward commercial use are designed to perform only one or two functions. A bicep-curl machine, for example, can only be used to

exercise the biceps. In comparison, a bar and several hundred pounds of plates can allow you to perform movements for just about every muscle in your body. So, free weights give you more variety per dollar.

3. It is safe to say that when it comes to free weights, "one size fits all." Indeed, free weights can accommodate just about everyone regardless of their size from your largest wrestler to your smallest. On the other hand, athletes who are at an extreme in terms of skeletal height and/or limb length may not be able to fit properly on some machines. For this reason, machines present a major drawback for many adolescents who wish to strength train.

4. Balancing free weights requires a greater involvement of synergistic muscles. Keep in mind, though, that the significance of this remains unclear. Ken Mannie, the Strength and Conditioning Coach at Michigan State, points out that "the rate and level at which [the synergistic muscles] act merit additional study."

Advantages of Machines

Machines have the following advantages over free weights:

1. Some exercises can only be done with machines including hip abduction, hip adduction, hip flexion, leg curl, leg extension and lat pulldown as well as those for the neck. These exercises and others have a valuable role in a comprehensive weight-training program.

2. Most machines can provide variable resistance. As an exercise is performed, the biomechanical leverage of your skeletal system changes – which makes the movement feel easier in some positions and harder in others. A properly designed machine automatically varies the resistance to match the changes in your biomechanical leverage. In positions of inferior leverage (and inferior strength), the machine creates a mechanical advantage and a lower level of resistance; as your skeletal system moves into a position of superior leverage (and superior strength), the machine creates a mechanical disad-

vantage and a higher level of resistance. The end result is greater muscular effort throughout the range of motion (ROM). During a typical free-weight exercise, there is adequate resistance for your muscles in their weakest positions but not enough in their strongest positions. Because of this, the amount of resistance that you can use is limited to that which you can handle in your position of least leverage. There are, however, a few free-weight exercises that provide somewhat adequate resistance throughout most of the ROM including wrist flexion/extension, shoulder shrug and calf raise.

3. As noted previously, you are required to balance the resistance when using free weights. Having to do this can be viewed as a drawback. Some athletes – particularly those who have very little experience in weight training – might worry more about balancing the resistance than about performing the movement properly. Furthermore, you are likely to spend excessive energy in balancing the weight. With most machines, the weight is already balanced for you so that you will be able to concentrate on the proper performance of the exercise. By not involving synergistic muscles when the weight is balanced, machines can also work the target muscles to a greater degree.

4. Workouts are generally more time-efficient when machines are used. Some wrestlers do not have an abundance of extra time to spend in the weight room – especially during the season. The resistance on machines can be set by simply moving a selector pin rather than by fiddling around changing plates.

5. In general, machines provide direct resistance over a greater ROM compared to a similar free-weight exercise. A machine pullover, for example, can provide direct resistance over as much as 270 degrees ROM around your shoulder joint. By comparison, a barbell or dumbbell pullover provides only about 100 degrees of direct resistance for the same musculature – that is, your latissimus dorsi or, simply, your "lats." Therefore, a pull-

over done on a machine is much more efficient than a pullover done with free weights because the targeted muscles are exercised over a greater ROM. This holds true for just about all machine exercises compared to their free-weight counterparts.

6. Many free-weight exercises do not provide the targeted muscles with an adequate stretch. For instance, a barbell bench press restricts the stretching of your chest muscles – you could stretch them further but are unable to do so because the bar must stop at your chest. Almost all machine-type bench presses utilize movement arms with an opening for your chest. This enables you to obtain a greater stretch so that you do not compromise your flexibility. It should be noted that performing free-weight exercises with dumbbells can allow you to obtain a better stretch than with a barbell.

7. Machines are more practical than free weights during rehabilitation. Suppose that you injured your left knee. Many free-weight exercises would be quite difficult or uncomfortable (if not impossible) to perform. However, you could still train your entire torso, your right leg and possibly even both hips if you have access to machines. You could even continue to exercise on most machines with very little discomfort even if your arm or leg was in a cast. For instance, if your wrist was casted such that you were unable to grasp a barbell or dumbbell, you could still perform many upper-body exercises on machines including the "pec dec," pullover and lateral raise.

8. For reasons of safety, any barbell exercise that involves lifting a weight over your head – such as a bench press or a seated press – should only be done with a spotter. With machines, a spotter is rarely needed because it is virtually impossible to get pinned underneath a bar or stuck with a weight in a compromising position. It should be noted that overhead lifting can be done with dumbbells without requiring a spotter for safety.

SO, WHICH ARE BETTER?

There are advantages to both free weights and machines. No doubt, some coaches and athletes will always prefer one more than the other and that's all right as long as the favoritism is not born out of misconceptions or commercial bias. Remember, the bottom line is that your muscles do not respond one way with free weights and another way with machines. To quote Dan Riley, the Strength and Conditioning Coach of the Houston Texans who has spent more than 20 years in the National Football League, "The equipment used is not the key to maximum gains. It's how you use the equipment."

So, keep an open mind when it comes to selecting equipment for weight training. If you do not have a preference, then vary your workouts with free weights *and* machines.

DUMBBELL TRAINING

A dumbbell is essentially a shorter version of a barbell that is intended for use with one hand. There are two main advantages of using dumbbells in your training.

One advantage is that dumbbells can provide variety to your routine. Since every exercise that can be performed with a barbell can also be performed with dumbbells, every barbell exercise has a dumbbell counterpart that can be used as an alternative movement. In addition, you have the added option of being able to use a different grip with dumbbells. For example, you can do a seated press with dumbbells using a traditional grip (similar to that which would be used with a barbell) as well as a "parallel grip" (with your palms facing each other).

Another advantage of using dumbbells is that each of your limbs must work independently of the other. Most individuals are often stronger (and more flexible) on one side of their body than the other. Usually, this is not a significant difference. But when there is a gross difference in the strength between limbs, the use of dumbbells is highly recommended. This is also an important consideration for rehabilitative strength training. In this case, an individual may even have to work one limb at a time while using a lighter weight for the weaker limb.

In short, the advantages of dumbbells are pure and simple: variety and an independent workload.

BODY PARTS AND EXERCISES

The following is a list of body parts (muscles) and exercises that can be performed with dumbbells to address those areas:

Hips

A multiple-joint movement that you can do with dumbbells for your hips is the deadlift. This exercise also provides work for the muscles of the upper legs (the quadriceps and hamstrings) as well as the lower back. When dumbbells are used in this exercise, it provides one major advantage over its barbell counterpart: You can perform the deadlift more comfortably because the bar does not ride up and down your shins.

Calves

You can address the backs of your lower legs by doing a calf raise in a standing position using a dumbbell for resistance. Here is a brief description of this exercise: Hold the dumbbell in one hand and stand on something that is solid and at least several inches high. Hold onto a piece of equipment with your other hand to maintain your balance and position your legs so that the balls of your feet are on the edge. To do the exercise, keep your legs straight and rise up onto your toes as high as possible. Pause briefly in this mid-range position (your ankles extended) and then lower the weight under control to the starting position (your heels near the floor) to ensure a proper stretch. If you find that this is too easy, simply do the exercise with one leg at a time.

Chest

There are three multiple-joint movements that you can perform with dumbbells to emphasize different parts of your chest: the bench press (middle part), decline press (lower part) and incline press (upper part). These dumbbell exercises can be executed with a traditional bench-press grip or with a "parallel grip." Multiple-joint movements for the chest also provide indirect work for your anterior deltoids (on the front part of your shoulders) and triceps. The bent-arm fly with dumbbells – a single-joint movement – can be used to target your chest and anterior deltoids without involving your triceps. Also keep in mind that you can perform the bent-arm fly with dumbbells on supine (flat), decline and incline benches to work different parts of your chest.

Upper Back

Unfortunately, dumbbell exercises for the upper back (the "lats") are not very plentiful. As a matter of fact, there are only two worthwhile exercises: the bent-over row and pullover. The bent-over row is a multiple-joint movement that works your lats, biceps and forearms. You will be able to perform the bent-over row more comfortably and with better technique if you do it with one arm at a time. The pullover with dumbbells – a single-joint movement – allows you to isolate your lats without involving your biceps and forearms.

Shoulders

There are a multitude of exercises that you can do with dumbbells for your shoulders. This is good news, since your shoulders are made up of 11 different muscles. The seated press is a multiple-joint movement that involves your anterior deltoids and triceps. The three parts of the deltoids – the anterior (on the front), middle (on the side) and posterior (on the back) – can be isolated with dumbbells by doing the front, lateral and bent-over raises, respectively. Two dumbbell exercises are particularly useful for targeting your trapezius (or "traps"): the upright row and shoulder shrug. The upright row is a multiple-joint movement that also involves your biceps and forearms; the shoulder shrug is a single-joint movement that allows you to isolate your trapezius. Finally, you can do internal and external rotation with dumbbells to exercise the deep muscles of your shoulder: the "internal rotators" (subscapularis and teres major) and "external rotators" (infraspinatus and teres minor).

Biceps

A generic term for exercises that target the biceps is the "bicep curl." You can do this exercise with dumbbells either standing upright or seated as well as on a "preacher-curl" bench.

Triceps

A generic term for exercises that target the triceps is the "tricep extension." You can do this exercise with dumbbells either standing upright or seated (a "French curl") as well as lying supine on a flat bench.

Forearms

Two basic exercises that you can perform with dumbbells for your forearms (or lower arms) are wrist flexion and wrist extension. Wrist flexion works the anterior (or front) portion of your forearms; wrist extension works the posterior (or back) portion of your forearms. A third exercise for your forearms that can be done with dumbbells is finger flexion. This is a simple yet highly effective exercise that targets your finger flexors – highly important muscles that relatively few individuals work directly. Here is a brief description of the exercise: Grasp a dumbbell in each hand. Hold the dumbbells at the sides of your body with your palms facing your legs and spread your feet about shoulder-width apart. Allow the dumbbells to roll down your hands to your fingertips. To do the exercise, keep your arms fairly straight and pull the dumbbells up to your thumbs. Pause briefly in this mid-range position (your fingers flexed) and then lower the dumbbells under control to the starting position (your fingers extended) to ensure an adequate stretch.

Abdominals

The side bend with a dumbbell is a very good exercise for training the obliques (the muscles on the sides of your abdomen). This exercise – which also targets the muscles of your lower back – involves lateral flexion of your torso.

Lower Back

An exercise that you can do with dumbbells to address your lower back is the stiff-leg deadlift. The execution is similar to that of a regular deadlift but – as the name suggests – the exercise is done with your legs "stiff" or almost straight. By not involving your legs during the exercise, you will limit the contribution of your quadriceps (although you may notice that your hips and hamstrings are still used to some degree). In terms of execution, you should hold the dumbbells in front of your body in roughly the same position as if you were using a barbell.

DON'T BE A DUMBBELL

Figure 13.1 is a summary of the dumbbell exercises that have been discussed. You can do an entire workout using dumbbells or simply intermingle them with other exercises. Regardless, using dumbbells offers several advantages and a large inventory of exercise options.

BODY PART	EXERCISE
Hips	Deadlift
Calves	Calf Raise
Chest	Bench Press
	Decline Press
	Incline Press
	Bent-Arm Fly
Upper Back	Bent-Over Row
	Pullover
Shoulders	Seated Press
	Shoulder Shrug
	Upright Row
	Bent-Over Raise
	Front Raise
	Lateral Raise
	External Rotation
	Internal Rotation
Biceps	Bicep Curl
Triceps	Tricep Extension
Forearms	Wrist Extension
	Wrist Flexion
	Finger Flexion
Abdominals	Side Bend
Lower Back	Stiff-Leg Deadlift

FIGURE 13.1: SUMMARY OF DUMBBELL EXERCISES

Chapter 14

WRESTLING CAMP 2002 Q&A

The Princeton University Wrestling Camp – directed by Head Coach Michael New – was held from July 8 - 11, 2002. This was the second year for the camp and, based upon the number of campers in attendance, it was deemed a success. On the Tuesday evening of camp week, I had the opportunity to speak to the campers about strength and conditioning for wrestling. A question-and-answer session made for some great discussions. What follows is a sampling of questions that the wrestlers asked about strength and conditioning along with my responses. (In crafting this into the format of a chapter, I have taken the liberty of including a bit more information than I gave the campers.)

Q: What do you think of ephedrine?

First of all, I am not a big fan of herbs or other nutritional supplements. I think that you can get all of the nutrients that you need from the foods that you eat as long as you are consuming a balanced diet that has sufficient calories. Remember, too, that the Food and Drug Administration does not regulate nutritional supplements for safety, effectiveness, purity or potency. Due to this lack of federal oversight, you really do not know exactly what is in the products. It is not uncommon for independent researchers to find ingredients in the products that were not listed on the labels. Some nutritional supplements may also contain contaminants – most likely from the manufacturing process – such as aluminum, lead, mercury and tin.

At any rate, ephedrine – also known as "ephedra" – is an over-the-counter herbal stimulant that is found in many cold and flu medications as well as supplements that are marketed for weight loss. Understand that ephedrine is an amphetamine-like compound that has many adverse side effects. For one thing, it increases your heart rate and blood pressure. Personally, I would not want to elevate my heart rate and blood pressure and then do any type of physical training. Other common side effects from ephedrine include dizziness and headaches. The use of ephedrine also increases the potential for dehydration and has been linked to seizures, strokes and heart attacks. Since the mid-1990s, the Food and Drug Administration has received *more than 800 reports* of adverse side effects related to the use of ephedrine – including *at least 50 deaths*. The National Collegiate Athletic Association [NCAA] and the National Football League [NFL] have banned the use of supplements that contain ephedrine.

Q: What is the best thing to eat after a workout?

During intense activity – whether it is strength training, conditioning or practicing – your body's preferred source of energy is carbohydrates which circulate in your bloodstream as glucose and are stored in your liver and muscles as glycogen. It stands to reason, then, that your post-workout meal should contain foods that are high in carbohydrates. Now, keep in mind that there are different types of carbohydrates. After an intense workout, it is best to consume foods that have a high Glycemic Index such as bananas, watermelons, waffles, rice cakes, corn flakes, white rice, baked potatoes, white bread and buckwheat pancakes.

There is some evidence to suggest that combining the carbohydrates with a small amount of protein can expedite recovery by improving the rate at which your glycogen stores are replenished. However, it appears that simply increasing the quantity of post-workout carbohydrates will have the same results. Nonetheless, consuming a small amount of protein following an intense workout may aid in the repair of muscle tissue. Finally, it is also important to rehydrate after a workout. You should consume about 16 ounces of water for every pound of bodyweight that you lose during your training.

Incidentally, foods consumed prior to a workout should also

be high in carbohydrates. But this time, the foods should have a low Glycemic Index such as grapefruit, milk, pears, plain pizza, apples, apple juice, spaghetti, oranges, macaroni, oatmeal and orange juice. The idea here is to consume foods that are easily digested and do not elevate your blood sugar.

Q: Is there a certain sequence that I should use to train my muscles?

Yes. You should begin your workout by training your neck. The reason for this is that – from the standpoint of injury prevention – the neck muscles are the most important ones in wrestling. An injury to your knee is one thing. But an injury to your neck could have catastrophic results.

After this, you should exercise your muscles from largest to smallest. Your hips and legs have the largest – and most powerful – muscles in your body. Besides having a huge amount of muscle mass, your hips and legs are involved in many techniques on the wrestling mat. Train your hips first, followed by your upper legs and then your lower legs. In other words, start with your hips and work your way down to your ankles. Assuming a total-body workout, you should next train the major muscles of your torso: your chest, upper back (or "lats") and shoulders. Once you have done this, you can train your upper and lower arms. You would not want to train your biceps before you do an exercise for your upper back such as the lat pulldown. That would be a great sequence for your biceps but your upper back – which is the target of the exercise – will not get enough stimulation. Nor would you want to train your triceps before you do an exercise for your chest such as the bench press. That would be a great sequence for your triceps but your chest – which is the target of the exercise – will be having a picnic. After this, you should train your mid-section. This includes your abdominals and lower back.

In short, you should address your muscles in the following sequence: neck, hips, legs, torso and mid-section.

Q: What is the best lifting program for wrestling?

I think that it is necessary to first understand the reasons why you should be strength training. And these reasons may be different from what you might think. The main purpose of strength training is to decrease your injury potential. The operative word here is "potential." Just because you improve your strength does not mean that you will never get hurt. Often, injuries are simply a matter of being in the wrong place at the wrong time. But if you can strengthen your muscles, connective tissues and bones to tolerate more stress, you will certainly reduce your risk of getting injured. And if you did suffer an injury, it will be less severe and you will recover from it more quickly. The second purpose for strength training is to increase your performance potential. Again, the operative word here is "potential." Just because you improve the strength of your muscles does not mean that you will automatically be a better wrestler. You must still practice and perfect your wrestling skills in order to learn how to apply your increased strength on the wrestling mat.

Quick story: Greg Parker, our 174-pounder who finished second at this year's [2002] NCAA Championships, did not lift weights in high school. He said that because of this, he had to perfect his wrestling technique as much as possible. When he arrived at Princeton University, he began lifting weights on a regular basis and has dramatically improved his muscular size and strength. Now, he can execute his moves more easily and also do moves that were previously difficult to do.

Having said that, there is really no "best" or optimal program for wrestling. Many types of programs can give you favorable results. The program that you ultimately choose to do should be based upon five criteria.

Number one: The program must be productive. It does not make sense for you to invest time in a program if it does not produce meaningful results. A program will be productive as long as it is based upon scientific research, common sense and deductive reasoning not unfounded advice, wild speculation and wishful thinking.

Number two: The program must be comprehensive. A program should address all of the major muscles in your body – not just the "showy" ones. In addition, a comprehensive program is one that is performed year-round – including throughout the off-season and the in-season. Training during the season is especially important since this is when you need to be at your best in terms of strength and conditioning.

Number three: The program must be practical. In other words, it must be relatively easy to understand. In some instances, programs are grossly overcomplicated and correspondingly confusing. Strength training need not be complicated.

Number four: The program must be efficient. It should produce the *maximum* possible results in the *minimum* amount of time. A program that requires you to lift weights for lengthy periods of time or more than several workouts per week is not an efficient use of your time . . . nor is it necessary. You should *invest* time in the weight room not *spend* time.

And number five: The program must be safe. At first glance, many programs can look quite appealing. Closer inspection, however, may reveal that the programs are highly questionable in terms of safety. There is no need whatsoever to perform potentially dangerous activities or exercises in the weight room.

So the program that you choose for wrestling should be productive, comprehensive, practical, efficient and safe.

Q: What are some good exercises for the neck?

Great question. As I said earlier, your neck muscles are the most important ones in your body in terms of preventing catastrophic injury. If you sustain a severe neck injury, you could become paralyzed. So it is critical that you strengthen your neck.

If you have access to a neck machine, you are fortunate. But if you do not, there is no need to worry. The thing to understand is that you do not need a $3,000 machine to train your neck. You can do manual-resistance exercises for your neck with the aid of a partner. Two excellent exercises are neck flexion and neck extension.

To position yourself for neck flexion, lie face up on the back pad of a bench and place your feet flat on the floor. Position your head over the end of the back pad, interlock your fingers and place them across your chest. The spotter should stand alongside your head and apply resistance against your chin with one hand and your forehead with the other. To do the exercise, pull your head as close to your chest as possible as the spotter applies resistance evenly throughout the full range of motion. Pause briefly in this mid-range position with your chin near your chest and then resist as the spotter pushes your head back to the starting position with your head hanging down to provide an adequate stretch.

To position yourself for neck extension, lie face down on the back pad of a bench and place your hands and feet on the floor. Position your head over the end of the back pad. The spotter should stand alongside your head and apply resistance against the back of your head. To do the exercise, extend your head backward as far as possible as the spotter applies resistance evenly throughout the full range of motion. Pause briefly in this mid-range position with your neck extended and then resist as the spotter pushes your head back to the starting position with your chin near your chest to ensure an adequate stretch.

Q: What do you think about isometrics?

Basically, isometrics are exercises in which you push or pull against an immovable resistance. Their popularity increased enormously in the middle of the 1900s after two German researchers – Hettinger and Muller – released their findings that showed the benefits of isometrics.

Can you get stronger by doing isometrics? Absolutely. But isometrics have several disadvantages. For one thing, isometrics increase your blood pressure beyond what would be normally encountered when strength training with conventional methods. In addition, isometrics do not involve full-range repetitions. As a result, any increases in strength are specific to the joint angle being worked plus or minus a small number of degrees. And since isometrics do not involve full-range repetitions, your muscles do not receive any stretch at all. So after a while of doing a program of isometrics, you will likely lose flexibility.

Q: What is the best way to lose fat and still have energy?

This is an interesting question. In order to lose fat, you must produce a caloric deficit where the calories that you expend or "burn" are greater than the calories that you consume or eat. Now, the caloric deficit should not be more than about 500 - 1,000 calories below your normal daily caloric needs. If you lose more than about 1% of your bodyweight per week, it is likely that some of the weight loss will be the result of decreased lean-body mass and/or water rather than body fat. However, if the weight loss is less than about 1% of your bodyweight per week and is the result of a rigorous training program in conjunction with a reduced caloric intake, then it will probably be in the form of decreased body fat. You can produce a caloric deficit three ways: By decreasing your caloric consumption, increasing your caloric expenditure or doing a combination of the two. In fact, proper weight loss should be a blend of consuming less calories and expending more calories.

If your caloric intake is too low or restrictive, then you will not have much energy. So the key to losing fat while still having energy is to create a caloric deficit by decreasing your caloric consumption and increasing your caloric expenditure in moderate amounts.

Q: Why are some people just naturally bigger and stronger than others?

The reason for this is because each person – except for identical twins – is unique with a different genetic potential for achieving muscular size and strength. Some people are predisposed toward developing a high level of muscular size and strength; others are not as fortunate. For the most part, you cannot change the qualities that you have inherited from your ancestors. Inherited characteristics that greatly influence your muscular size and strength include your predominant muscle-fiber type and the insertion points of your tendons. But regardless of your genetic destiny, your goal should be to realize your physical potential as a wrestler.

Chapter 15

PERSPECTIVES ON PERIODIZATION AND PLYOMETRICS

Coaches and athletes are always looking for ways to improve performance on the wrestling mat. And there is no shortage of methods that are purported to develop various physiological functions such as strength, speed, power and explosiveness. Two popular methods of training are examined here: periodization and plyometrics.

PERIODIZATION

Also referred to as "cycling," periodization is a theoretical schedule of pre-planned workouts that has been popularized by competitive weightlifters as their preferred method of training to peak for a one-repetition maximum (1-RM) during their contests. Essentially, the idea is to change or "cycle" program variables such as the number of sets and repetitions, the workloads (which are based upon percentages of a 1-RM) and the recovery intervals between the sets/exercises. These variables are manipulated during rigidly defined "phases" of training which usually are designated as "hypertrophy," "basic strength," "strength-power," "peaking," "maintenance" and "active rest." It is thought that by manipulating the variables, athletes can selectively target specific physiological functions.

Here is a relatively simple example of a classic (linear) model of periodization that is divided into two seven-week "cycles" or "periods" (to supposedly develop strength and power): During the first three weeks of each cycle, wrestlers are required to do 2 - 3 sets of 8 - 10 repetitions in each exercise with 50 - 70% of their 1-RMs; during the fourth and fifth weeks of each cycle, they must do 3 - 4 sets of 6 repetitions in each exercise with 70 - 85% of their 1-RMs; and during the sixth and seventh weeks of each cycle, they must do 3 - 5 sets of 1 - 4 repetitions in each exercise with 85 - 95% of their 1-RMs.

There are several issues and concerns relating to the use of periodization. Perhaps first and foremost is the fact that there is no legitimate scientific evidence to support the wild claim that doing different numbers of sets and repetitions with different percentages of a 1-RM while taking different intervals of recovery between sets will specifically influence hypertrophy, strength, strength-power or anything else.

Second, periodization is overly – and unnecessarily – complicated and correspondingly confusing. The use of pseudoscientific terminology coupled with pre-planned workouts that specify inflexible instructions to vary the sets, repetitions, workloads and recovery intervals in rigidly defined phases adds to the confusion. Equally confusing is the notion of "active rest" – a contradiction in terms if there ever was one. Strength training is actually quite simple: Overload the muscles by increasing the resistance and/or repetitions from one workout to the next.

Third, periodization is far too inflexible because of the precise nature of pre-planned workouts. The reality is that wrestlers often get sick or injured and are forced to miss workouts. In the event of a missed workout, do they renew their training according to their pre-planned schedule? If not, at what point in the pre-planned schedule do they resume? Essentially, "periodization" is a sexy word for "variety." But incorporating variety into a program – which is certainly important – can be done as needed in a manner that is far less regimented and much more informal.

Fourth, periodization requires all athletes to perform specific numbers of repetitions with certain percentages of their 1-RMs. For instance, wrestlers might be required to do 8 repetitions with 70% of their 1-RMs. Because of wide variations in muscular endurance, however, such a prescription might be far too easy for some and literally impossible for others. Therefore, pre-planned workouts that demand the same number of repetitions be done with a specific percentage of a maximal load are only effective for the relatively small segment of the population that has inherited a particular level of muscular endurance that corresponds exactly to the specifications and parameters of the training schedule.

Fifth, periodization makes some sense for competitive weightlifters since – for the most part – they only peak for two or three contests a year. But it makes little sense for other athletes such as wrestlers who might have to peak once or twice a week for three or four months. Indeed, for what matches do they peak? Isn't every one important? Imagine a wrestler saying apologetically, "Sorry about my performance today, coach, but I'm not scheduled to peak in my Strength-Power Phase for two more weeks." Remember, too, that references to the training methods or techniques of competitive weightlifters are irrelevant and, therefore, do not apply to any athletes other than competitive weightlifters. The question that a wrestler must ask is, "Am I training to become a better wrestler or a better weightlifter?"

To summarize: Besides being confusing, trying to implement periodization with athletes other than competitive weightlifters is impractical, irrelevant, illogical and unnecessary. There are other ways to address a wrestler's needs that are considerably less complicated as well as more practical, relevant and logical.

PLYOMETRICS

Since the mid-1960s, plyometrics have been romantically endorsed as a way to "bridge the gap" between strength and speed. In the United States, the first reference to these types of exercises in athletic literature appears to have been in 1966 by the Soviet author Yuri Verhoshanski (whose surname has also been spelled "Verkhoshansky"). The term "plyometrics," however, seems to have been coined in 1975 by Fred Wilt who was an American track and field coach.

Plyometrics apply to any exercise or jumping drill that uses the myotatic (or stretch) reflex of a muscle. This particular reflex is triggered when a muscle is pre-stretched prior to a muscular contraction, resulting in a more powerful movement than would otherwise be possible. Just before lifting an opponent, for example, a wrestler bends at the hips and knees. This "countermovement" pre-stretches the hip and leg muscles allowing the wrestler to generate more force than if the lift was performed without first bending the hips and knees. Plyometrics for the lower body include bounding, hopping and various box drills such as depth jumping (in which an athlete steps off a box and, upon landing, immediately does a vertical jump); plyometrics for the upper body include ballistic (or "drop") push-ups and often incorporate medicine balls to induce the stretch reflex.

Understand that the use of plyometrics has been highly controversial for quite some time. It is important to know that most of the support for plyometrics is based upon anecdotal – not scientific – evidence. The truth of the matter is that there is little unbiased research that convincingly and consistently proves plyometrics are effective.

Although some research has shown that plyometrics are effective, roughly an equal amount of research has shown that they are no more effective than regular strength-training or jumping activities when it comes to improving strength, speed, power, explosiveness or any other physiological function. For instance, a study that involved 26 subjects found no significant improvement in the vertical jump in those who performed depth jumps two times per week. In a study that involved 38 subjects, researchers found no significant difference in the vertical jump between a group that trained with an isokinetic leg press and a group that trained with depth jumps. In a study that involved 44 subjects (in two different experiments), researchers concluded that depth jumps (of varying heights) are no more effective than "other more common training methods" for improving leg strength and the vertical jump. A study that involved 50 subjects found no significant differences in the 40-yard dash and vertical jump between one group that did strength training and two groups that did plyometrics. A study that involved 31 subjects showed no significant differences in dynamic leg strength and leg power between one group that performed maximum vertical jumps from ground level and two groups that performed depth jumps from different heights. And in a study that involved 24 subjects, researchers found no significant differences in the vertical jump, leg press and peak power of the quadriceps between a group that performed a strength-training program and a group that performed a strength-training program and plyometrics.

One other bit of research deserves special note: In a study that involved 30 subjects, researchers found that as the height of the depth jump *increased* the performance in the vertical jump and maximal vertical power output *decreased* in a linear fashion. Actually, the greatest performances were produced by depth jumping from a height of only *4.72 inches.* Given this information, it is difficult to understand why depth jumping is even done.

So while the mechanical output of a muscle is certainly increased by the pre-stretch mechanism, it does not necessarily follow that a physiological or neurological adaptation/alteration occurs. Even if there was indisputable evidence that plyometrics were an effective way to improve strength, speed, power and explosiveness – or anything else – it is extremely important to consider the risks. Frankly, the potential for injury from plyometrics is enormous. A large number of strength and fitness professionals have questioned the safety of plyometrics for many years. When performing plyometrics, the musculoskeletal system is exposed to repetitive trauma and high-impact forces. The extreme biomechanical loading places an inordinate amount of stress on the muscles, bones and connective tissues. Research has suggested that the stress from the impact forces increases the potential for injury. This is particularly true of plyometrics that have a large vertical component such as depth jumping.

The most common plyometric-related injuries in the lower body are patellar tendinitis ("jumper's knee"), stress fractures, shin splints, muscle strains, heel bruises and sprains of the knee and ankle. Other potential injuries include compression fractures, ruptured tendons and meniscal (cartilage) damage. Another area that is highly susceptible to injury from plyometrics is the lower back. Several studies have found that depth jumping results in "spinal shrinkage" – that is, a loss of stature – presumably from compression of the intervertebral discs. It is reasonable to think that decreases in the height of the discs increases the potential for injury to the spine. And performing depth jumps from greater heights or with added weight significantly increases the impact forces and spinal shrinkage. Doing so may also cause athletes to alter their landing strategies as a protective mechanism thereby increasing the potential for other injuries. Young athletes are especially vulnerable because their musculoskeletal systems are relatively immature.

When aerobic dancing was introduced years ago, most fitness enthusiasts eagerly accepted this activity with little or no reservation. Within a short period of time, untold numbers of participants suffered injuries that were directly attributable to the high-impact forces that were absorbed by their musculoskeletal systems. The concerns about these inherent dangers ushered in the development and acceptance of low-impact aerobics. If a multitude of injuries resulted from jumping up and down several *inches*, how many injuries can be expected from jumping up and down several *feet*? Also consider this: Most authorities recommend that athletes should stretch under control without any bouncing or ballistic movements to reduce their risk of injury. The fact that plyometrics are an extremely violent form of stretching is a blatant contradiction to these safety concerns.

It is no surprise, then, that many individuals in the sportsmedical community view plyometrics as "an injury waiting to happen." According to Dr. Ken Leistner – who has treated his share of injuries in his New York office – plyometrics "are not safe under any circumstances, nor for any particular athlete, no matter how 'advanced' he or she may be." Adds Dr. Leistner, " . . . plyometrics are dangerous stuff and it is not fair, right or ethical for a coach to impose plyometrics on his or her athletes. Plyometrics are dangerous in themselves and will also do things to the body that will increase the probability of injuries during future events."

Before plyometrics can be accepted as an appropriate method of training, research must show that they are effective and safe on a more convincing and consistent basis. At this point in time, a compelling number of scientific studies have found that plyometrics are no more effective than regular strength-training and jumping activities. Moreover, plyometrics carry an unreasonably – and unjustifiably – high risk of injury.

That being said, it is important to understand that many plyometric drills are actually nothing more than glorified agility drills that are intended to improve specific skills, kinesthetic awareness and anaerobic conditioning. When these drills have a small vertical component and involve a low amount of impact forces, they are an effective and safe method of training. But when these drills have a large vertical component and involve a high amount of impact forces that aggressively pre-stretch muscles in an attempt to make the stretch reflex more responsive, they are an ineffective and dangerous method of training.

Wrestlers can improve their strength, speed, power and explosiveness in a much safer manner by simply practicing their wrestling skills and techniques in the same way that they are used on the mat and by strengthening their major muscle groups, especially the hips and legs.

Sooner or later, jumping off a plyometrics box will send you limping to a doctor's office. The bottom line: Look before you leap.

Chapter 16
CALORIC CONTRIBUTIONS AND NEEDS

Proper nutrition plays a critical role in your capacity to wrestle at optimal levels. You can improve your nutritional skills by understanding the caloric contributions of the various nutrients and knowing your caloric needs.

CALORIC CONTRIBUTIONS

Everything that you do requires energy. The energy is obtained through the foods (or nutrients) that you consume and is measured in calories (which, technically, are units of heat).

Three macronutrients – carbohydrates, protein and fat – furnish you with calories, albeit in different amounts. Carbohydrates and protein yield four calories per gram (cal/g). Fat is the most concentrated form of energy, containing nine cal/g. Armed with this information, you can determine the caloric contributions for each of the three energy-providing macronutrients in any food – provided that you know how many grams of each macronutrient are in a serving.

As an example, consider a snack food such as Fritos® Brand Original Corn Chips (Frito-Lay, Incorporated). Examining the nutrition label reveals that a one-ounce serving of this product contains 15 grams of carbohydrates, 2 grams of protein and 10 grams of fat. To find the exact number of calories that are supplied by each macronutrient, simply multiply its number of grams per serving by its corresponding energy yield. In this example, each serving of the food has 60 calories from carbohydrates [15 g x 4 cal/g], 8 calories from protein [2 g x 4 cal/g] and 90 calories from fat [10 g x 9 cal/g]. Therefore, this food has a total of 158 calories per serving (which is rounded up to

160 on the nutrition label). As you can see, this product has 50% more grams of carbohydrates than fat (15 compared to 10) – yet nearly 57% of the calories (90 of the 158) are furnished by fat. Moreover, consuming the entire contents of the 2.5-ounce bag will contribute 25 grams of fat – or 225 calories from fat – to your caloric budget.

Compare this to Baked Lays® Potato Crisps, another snack food by the same manufacturer. A one-ounce serving of this product has 23 grams of carbohydrates, 2 grams of protein and 1.5 grams of fat. Each serving of this food contains 92 calories from carbohydrates [23 g x 4 cal/g], 8 calories from protein [2 g x 4 cal/g] and 13.5 calories from fat [1.5 g x 9 cal/g]. So this food has a total of 113.5 calories per serving (which is rounded down to 110 on the nutrition label). This particular product, then, has more than 15 times as many grams of carbohydrates than fat (23 compared to 1.5) – and only 11.9% of the calories (13.5 of the 113.5) are supplied by fat. Furthermore, consuming 2.5 ounces of this product will add a mere 3.75 grams of fat – or 33.75 calories from fat – to your caloric budget.

Knowing the different caloric contributions of the macronutrients is also helpful in understanding information about fat content on the packaging of a product that could easily be misinterpreted. Case in point: A package that proclaims a product to be "99% fat free" means that it is 99% fat free by weight, not by calories. How critical is this distinction? Placing one gram of fat into 99 grams of water forms a product that, by weight, is "99% fat free." But since water has no calories, this particular "99% fat free" product would actually be – in terms of calories – 100% fat.

Although the preceding example was hypothetical, the fact is that this discrepancy actually occurs on the package of many products. Here are four illustrations of real products:

- A package of Hershey®'s Chocolate Drink (Hershey® Foods Corporation) states that it is "99% fat free." As would be expected, this leads many consumers to believe that a mere 1% of its calories come from fat. In reality, one serving of this product (eight ounces) has

129 calories of which 9 are from fat – meaning that it is 6.98% fat. (The numbers on the nutrition label are rounded up to 130 calories per serving with 10 calories from fat.)

- A package of Black Bear of the Black Forest™ Gourmet Cooked Ham (Black Bear Enterprises, Incorporated) notes that it is "98% fat free." Naturally, this prompts many consumers to think that only 2% of its calories are derived from fat. In actuality, one serving of this product (two ounces) has 49 calories of which 9 are from fat – meaning that it is 18.36% fat. (The values on the nutrition label are rounded up to 50 calories per serving with 10 calories from fat.)

- A package of Black Bear of the Black Forest™ Barbeque Flavor Breast of Chicken states that it is "96% fat free." This, of course, leads many consumers to conclude that only 4% of its calories come from fat. In reality, one serving of this product (two ounces) has 66 calories of which 18 are from fat – meaning that it is 27.27% fat. (The numbers on the nutrition label are rounded up to 70 calories per serving with 20 calories from fat.)

- A package of Oscar Mayer® Dinner Ham (Oscar Mayer Foods) notes that it is "96% fat free." Again, this leads many consumers to believe that only 4% of its calories are from fat. In actuality, one serving of this product (three ounces) has 83 calories of which 27 are from fat – meaning that it is 32.53% fat. (The values on the nutrition label are rounded down to 80 calories per serving with 25 calories from fat.)

While the percentages of fat calories for these four products are not terribly bad, it is certainly a far cry from how the percentages on the package can be interpreted.

CALORIC NEEDS

Your need for calories (or energy) is determined by several factors such as your age, gender, size, body composition, metabolic rate and level of activity. During a resting state, your caloric requirements can be established precisely by both direct and indirect calorimetry. Direct calorimetry measures the heat produced by the body in a small, insulated chamber; indirect calorimetry calculates the heat given off by the body based upon the amount of oxygen that is consumed and carbon dioxide that is produced. Unfortunately, both of these methods can be expensive and impractical for most people. For a quick and reasonably accurate estimate of your daily caloric needs, the U. S. Department of Agriculture suggests that you multiply your bodyweight by a number that corresponds to your approximate level of activity. Essentially, this number represents your energy requirements in calories per pound of bodyweight (cal/lb). For females, the values are 14 if the woman is sedentary, 18 if she is moderately active and 22 if she is very active; for males, the factors are 16, 21 and 26, respectively. For instance, a 150-pound male who is very active requires about 3,900 calories per day (cal/day) to meet his energy needs [150 lb x 26 cal/lb]. In other words, this individual needs to consume approximately 3,900 calories per day to maintain his current bodyweight of 150 pounds. Although this calculation has gray areas – such as the characterization of the term "moderately active" – it still results in a fairly good estimate.

Once you have estimated your caloric budget, you can determine how many of these calories should come from carbohydrates, protein and fat. Using the previous example, someone who requires about 3,900 cal/day should consume roughly 633.75 grams of carbohydrates [3,900 cal/day x 0.65 ÷ 4 cal/g], 146.25 grams of protein [3,900 cal/day x 0.15 ÷ 4 cal/g] and 86.67 grams of fat [3,900 cal/day x 0.20 ÷ 9 cal/g]. Note that these numbers are based upon a diet for an active lifestyle that consists of 65% carbohydrates, 15% protein and 20% fat.

Chapter 17

PRE- AND POST-ACTIVITY FOODS/FUELS

Proper nutrition has an important role in your ability to perform at maximal levels and to expedite your recovery. Clearly, your ability to fully recuperate after an exhaustive activity directly affects your future performance and intensity in your training. Knowing what foods/fluids to consume before and after vigorous activity is truly helpful in optimizing your performance.

PRE-ACTIVITY FOODS/FUELS

A meal consumed prior to an activity – that is, a wrestling match or training session – should accomplish several things such as removing your hunger pangs, readying your body with fuel for the upcoming activity and relaxing your psychological state. There is no food that you can consume before an activity that will directly improve your performance. But there are certain foods that you can consume before an activity that can impair your performance and, for that reason, should be avoided. For example, fats and meats are digested slowly and, therefore, should not be eaten prior to competing or training. Other foods to omit include those that are greasy, highly seasoned and flatulent (gas-forming) along with any specific foods that you may personally find distressful to your digestive system. If anything, the choices for your pre-activity meal should be almost bland, yet appetizing enough so that you want to eat it.

Prior to an activity, you should also avoid eating foods that cause a sharp increase in your levels of blood glucose. Here is why: In response to highly elevated blood-glucose levels, your body increases its blood-insulin levels to maintain a stable internal environment (known as "homeostasis"). As a result of this biochemical balancing, your blood glucose is sharply reduced. This leads to hypoglycemia (or "low blood sugar") which decreases the availability of blood glucose as a fuel and causes you to feel severely fatigued. Although this condition is usually temporary, it remains an important consideration.

The idea, then, is to consume foods that elevate or maintain your blood glucose without triggering a dramatic response by blood insulin. At one time, it was thought that simple carbohydrates (sugars) increase blood glucose more rapidly than complex carbohydrates (starches). A more recent trend of thought has been to consider the Glycemic Index (GI) of a food. The GI dates back to 1981 when it was conceptualized by a group of scientists as a way to help determine which foods were best for people with diabetes. Essentially, the GI is a system of quantifying the carbohydrates in foods based upon how they affect blood glucose. A value is assigned to a food that correlates to the magnitude of the increase in blood glucose. For instance, a food with a GI of 25 means that it elevates blood glucose to a level that is 25% as great as consuming the same amount of pure glucose. Incidentally, the GI is not related to portion size. So the GI is the same whether you consume 10 grams of a particular food or 110 grams. (The number of calories, of course, would differ according to the size of the portion.)

Before an activity, it is best to consume foods that are easy to digest and high in carbohydrates – specifically, those with a low GI. These foods help to keep your blood-glucose levels within a desirable range.

It is important not to simply assume that a sugary food raises blood glucose more than a starchy food. Indeed, honey (58) has a lower GI than a bagel (78) and, given these two options, would be a better choice for a pre-activity food. Foods with a relatively low GI include roasted peanuts (14), cherries (22), pure fructose (23), grapefruit (25), milk (34), pears (36), plain pizza (36), apples (38), apple juice (40), spaghetti (40), oranges (43), grapes (43), macaroni (46), oatmeal (55) and orange juice (55).

Water is perhaps the best liquid for you to drink before competing or training. Your fluid intake should be enough to guarantee optimal hydration during the activity.

The timing of your pre-activity meal is crucial to ensure that your digestive process does not impair your performance. Ideally, you should eat at least three hours prior to your activity. Obviously, you can control the timing of your meal such that it is not within three hours of a training session. Considering that the current rules for making weight require you to weigh in within this three-hour window of time, planning a meal prior to a wrestling match presents a greater challenge. With careful and disciplined preparation, however, you can effectively schedule the timing of your meal before a wrestling match. Michael New, the Head Wrestling Coach at Princeton University, offers this insight: "The best way to have fuel in your tank for your match is to be under the limit of your weight class several hours before weigh-ins. That way, you can eat some foods with a low GI and still make weight. And by the time that your match rolls around, you will be ready to wrestle. It all boils down to your mental discipline and planning."

In short, your pre-activity meal should be consumed more than three hours before training or competing and include foods that are familiar to you and are well tolerated – preferably carbohydrates with a low GI.

POST-ACTIVITY FOODS/FLUIDS

After an intense activity, proper nutrition accelerates your recovery and better prepares you for your next physical challenge. The idea is to replenish your depleted glycogen stores and to expedite your recovery process as soon as possible after a wrestling match or training session.

Following an activity, it is best to consume foods that are high in carbohydrates – specifically, those with a high GI. These foods will help to restore your muscle glycogen in the quickest fashion. Foods with a relatively high GI include bananas (60), table sugar (65), watermelon (72), waffles (76), rice cakes (77), Rice Krispies® (82), pretzels (83), corn flakes (84), white rice

(88), baked potatoes (93), white bread (95), glucose (100) and buckwheat pancakes (103).

Because your appetite is suppressed immediately after intense efforts, it may be more practical for you to initially consume fluids rather than solid food or a meal. Cold fluids also help to cool off your body. Commercial sports drinks can be excellent post-activity fluids. In terms of recovery, there are two important components of a sports drink: carbohydrates and electrolytes (sodium and potassium). All sports drinks are different, so you should read the nutrition labels to be sure of their exact contents. As an example, 12 ounces of Gatorade® Energy Drink (The Gatorade Company) has 78 grams of carbohydrates which provide 312 calories; the same amount of Gatorade® Thirst Quencher contains 21 grams of carbohydrates which provide 84 calories. Both products have adequate amounts of electrolytes and a high GI but vastly different levels of carbohydrates and calories.

According to Nancy Clark, M. S., R. D. – an internationally known sports nutritionist and author – you should consume 0.5 grams of carbohydrates per pound of your bodyweight (g/lb) within two hours of completing an intense activity. This should be repeated again within the next two hours. For instance, an individual who weighs 150 pounds needs to ingest about 75 grams of carbohydrates – or 300 calories of carbohydrates – within two hours after an intense activity and another 75 grams of carbohydrates during the next two hours [0.5 g/lb x 150 lb = 75 g].

Despite the efforts of the scientific and academic communities, myths concerning nutrition continue to abound. The following questions are often asked about nutrition (and supplements):

Q: Is it true that boron increases muscular size and strength?

Because of gross exaggerations by the supplement industry, individuals have used boron thinking that it will increase their muscular size and strength. One study that was frequently cited by the supplement industry showed that boron increased serum testosterone concentration up to 300%. What the promoters did not mention was that the subjects in this study were postmenopausal women whose testosterone levels were quite low. In fact, these women had not received adequate boron intake for the previous 119 days prior to the supplementation. In another study that involved 19 male bodybuilders (aged 20 - 27), the researchers concluded that boron supplementation had little effect on total testosterone, lean-body mass and muscular strength.

Q: Does caffeine affect my performance?

Caffeine – a stimulant of the central nervous system – is perhaps the most widely used drug in the world. It is a component of tea, coffee, chocolate and soft drinks as well as pills to lose weight and combat drowsiness. It has no significant nutritional value.

Interest in the use of caffeine as a performance enhancer –

or "ergogenic aid" – was primarily inspired by two studies that were published in the late 1970s. In those studies, caffeine produced significant improvements in endurance (in cycling). To date, numerous studies done in a laboratory setting have shown that caffeine increases performance in cycling and running for efforts that last roughly 5 - 20 minutes. But studies done outside a laboratory have found mixed results. At this time, it does not appear as if caffeine improves sprint performance (inside or outside a laboratory).

In low doses, caffeine can improve perception, increase alertness, decrease reaction time and lower anxiety levels. Keep in mind, though, that the effects are related to the dosage: Individual differences in the sensitivity and tolerance to caffeine certainly come into play.

When consumed in low doses, caffeine does not pose any serious risks for healthy individuals; when consumed in high doses, caffeine has the potential for many adverse side effects such as anxiety, jitters, tremors, inability to focus, gastrointestinal distress, diarrhea, insomnia, irritability and "withdrawal headache." Obviously, these side effects would be problematic for wrestlers (and other athletes as well). Since caffeine is a potent diuretic (which increases the production of urine), there has been some concern that it can increase the risk of dehydration – a major fear during physical activity, especially in a hot, humid environment. Although research has shown that caffeine does not pose any thermoregulatory risks, it is still an important consideration for wrestlers. Megadoses of caffeine have the potential for heart arrhythmias and mild hallucinations. Additionally, it is important to note that individuals who have pre-existing ulcer conditions and those who are prone to stomach distress should avoid caffeine. Finally, be aware that the United States Olympic Committee restricts the use of caffeine.

Q: Is it true that carbohydrates make you fat?

Absolutely not. The truth is that eating too much and exercising too little make you fat.

If anything, it is important for you to consume carbohydrates to fuel your athletic lifestyle. In fact, the primary function of carbohydrates is to supply you with energy – especially during intense exertions. The other two macronutrients that are sources of energy – protein and fat – have major limitations for athletes. Protein is actually your last resort since it is located in your muscles and if you are in a situation where you must rely on it as an energy source, then you are literally cannibalizing yourself; fat is an inefficient source of energy and, therefore, is preferred during low-intensity efforts when your body does not need to be efficient. In short, eliminating carbohydrates from your diet will inhibit your stamina and endurance.

Additionally, consuming too much protein and fat is associated with a greater risk of heart disease. Finally, remember that if you avoid carbohydrates, you also avoid foods with highly valuable nutrients such as fruits, vegetables and whole grains. This may lead to vitamin and mineral deficiencies. Clearly, carbohydrates are miscast villains.

Q: Are the product labels of herbs and other nutritional supplements accurate?

First of all, it is important to know that the Food and Drug Administration does not regulate herbs and other nutritional supplements for safety, effectiveness, purity or potency. As a result, you really do not know exactly what is in the products. Independent researchers have found ingredients in the products that were not listed on the labels. In one study, researchers analyzed 75 different nutritional products and found that seven (9.33%) contained substances that were not shown on the labels. Moreover, the active ingredient may be higher or lower than the amount listed on the label. Independent testing of 16 dehydroepiandrosterone (DHEA) products found that only eight (50%) contained the exact amount of DHEA that was stated on the labels and the actual levels varied *as much as 150%*. Amazingly, three (18.75%) of the 16 products did not contain any DHEA whatsoever. And some products may have ingredients that are truly bizarre. In a review of 311 advertisements for nutritional supplements, the researchers noted 235 unique ingredients including ecdysterone which is an insect hormone with no known use in humans. Herbs and other nutritional supplements may also contain contaminants such as aluminum, lead, mercury and tin.

Q: Is it safe to use herbs and other nutritional supplements that are natural?

Many herbs and other nutritional supplements are promoted as "natural." Because a product claims to be "natural" or have "natural" ingredients does not mean that it is necessarily safe. Dirt and urine are "natural" but that does not mean dirt is safe to eat and urine is safe to drink. The truth is that many "natural" substances can be quite harmful including high-potency doses of some vitamins, minerals and certain herbs. For instance, large doses of the natural stimulants found in ginseng can cause hypertension, insomnia, depression and skin blemishes. In addition, the medical literature contains numerous reports of severe liver toxicity linked to such widely used herbs as chaparral, comfrey and germander. There are similar safety concerns with high-potency enzymes, inert glandulars and animal extracts. One final point is that it is difficult to predict how some herbs interact with prescription and over-the-counter medications (as well as other nutritional supplements).

Finally, remember that many herbs and other nutritional supplements come with express or implied disease-related claims and are marketed for specific therapeutic purposes for which there may not be valid scientific proof. In one study, researchers reviewed all of the clinical trials that were published in 1966 - 1992 and compared the pertinent human and/or animal studies to that of the manufacturer's claims. It was found that 8 of the 19 products (42%) had no published scientific evidence to support the promotional claims. Another 6 of the 19 (32%) were judged as being marketed in a misleading manner. The fact of the matter is that the majority of herbs and other nutritional supplements have no recognized role in nutrition.

Q: Does whey protein increase muscle mass more than other proteins?

The supplement industry has claimed that whey protein promotes greater increases in muscle mass than other proteins. As support for this contention, the supplement industry has referenced a study in which the subjects significantly increased their bodyweights. What the promoters failed to mention was that the subjects in this study were starved rats. In the study, rats that were fed a whey-protein formula regained their lost weight faster than other rats that were fed a free-amino acid mixture. Obviously, it is difficult to extrapolate the influence of whey protein on starved rats to that of healthy humans.

Q: Is the food pyramid outdated?

Not really. Consuming an assortment of foods helps to ensure that you have obtained adequate amounts of carbohydrates, protein and fat along with sufficient quantities of vitamins and minerals. According to the U. S. Department of Agriculture and Department of Health and Human Services, a variety of daily foods should include an appropriate number of servings from these six food groups (with the servings in parentheses):

Bread, Cereal, Rice and Pasta (6 - 11)

Vegetable (3 - 5)

Fruit (2 - 4)

Milk, Yogurt and Cheese (2 - 3)

Meat, Poultry, Fish, Dry Beans, Eggs and Nuts (2 - 3)

Fats, Oils and Sweets (use sparingly)

The exact number of servings that are suitable for you is contingent upon your caloric (or energy) needs. Your caloric needs depend upon a number of factors, including your age, gender, size, body composition, metabolic rate and level of activity.

The recommendations for daily servings are based upon the Food Guide Pyramid that was introduced by the U. S. Department of Agriculture and Department of Health and Human Services in 1992. Two professors at the Harvard School of Public Health have suggested a new pyramid with different daily servings. While their proposal is interesting, it has yet to gain wide acceptance by the scientific and medical communities. There are also a number of other "pyramids" including the Asian Diet Pyramid, the Latin American Diet Pyramid, the Mayo Clinic Healthy Weight Pyramid, the Mediterranean Diet Pyramid and the Vegetarian Diet Pyramid. Despite the differences in the names, all of these pyramids have much in common. Bottom line: The daily servings that are currently recommended by the U. S. Department of Agriculture and Department of Health and Human Services are appropriate for wrestlers.

Q: Do wrestlers need to consume more than the RDA?

First published in 1943 and updated regularly, the Recommended Dietary Allowances (RDAs) were developed by the Food and Nutrition Board of the National Academy of Sciences/ National Research Council. The RDAs are set by first determining the "floor" below which deficiency occurs and then the "ceiling" above which harm occurs. A margin of safety is included in the RDAs to meet the requirements of nearly all healthy people. In fact, the RDAs are designed to cover the biological needs of 97.5% *of the population*. In other words, the RDAs exceed what most people require in order to meet the needs of those who have the highest requirements. So, the RDAs do not represent minimum standards. And failing to consume the recommended amounts does not necessarily indicate that you have a dietary deficiency.

Chapter 19

FAD DIETS: ATKINS AND ZONE

Make no mistake about it: Dieting is a multi-billion dollar business. As the term suggests, "fad" diets – like "fad" fashions – are those that are trendy for a while and then fade away only to resurface at some point in the future (sometimes with a new name). Fad diets have several things in common. First, they promise quick results – specifically, a rapid loss of weight. Second, they severely restrict one or more food groups or macronutrients. Third, they make big promises but offer little proof.

An endless stream of fad diets has been popular at one time or another. A partial list includes the Algoxyll Diet, Ayurvedic Diet, Bikini Diet, Blood Type Diet, Body Type Diet, Brain Chemistry Diet, Burn Rate Diet, Cabbage Soup Diet, Carbohydrate Addict's Diet, Detox Diet, Fit for Life Diet, Grapefruit Diet, Hollywood 48-Hour Miracle Diet, Ice Cream Diet, Immune Power Diet, LA Diet, Liver Cleansing Diet, Mediterranean Diet, Metabolic Typing Diet, New Beverly Hills Diet, No-Grain Diet, Omega Diet, Origin Diet, Paleo Diet, Peanut Butter Diet, Pritikin Diet, Protein Power Diet, RealAge Diet, Resolution Diet, Scarsdale Diet, Slim Forever Diet, Southampton Diet, South Beach Diet, Starch Blocker Diet, Stillman Diet, Sugar Buster's Diet, 30-Day Low-Carb Diet, Three-Day Diet, Tri-Color Diet and Warrior Diet. But perhaps the two most popular diets of all time are the Atkins Diet and the Zone Diet.

THE ATKINS DIET

Promoted by Dr. Robert Atkins, this diet calls for a food intake that is low in carbohydrates and high in protein and fats. Dr. Atkins endorsed the diet for more than 30 years until his death in April 2003 (from head injuries that were sustained in a fall on an icy sidewalk in New York City). Historically, diets seem to cycle in to and out of popularity and the Atkins Diet is no exception. Recently, the Atkins Diet has become fashionable again for two main reasons: (1) an article that was published in the *New York Times Magazine* by Gary Taubes and (2) the results of two independent studies that were published in the same issue of *The New England Journal of Medicine.*

In his article, Taubes enthusiastically endorsed the Akins Diet. However, many individuals in the scientific and medical communities responded to the article with quick and blistering rebuttals. Several who were quoted in the article claimed that Taubes had taken their words out of context or "tricked [them] all" into supporting the Atkins Diet; others claimed that he either disregarded or distorted their comments and provided information that was "incredibly misleading." One said that "he ignored research that did not agree with his conclusions." The shadow of doubt that this cast over his credibility renders the content of his article worthless.

The two studies that were published in a prestigious medical journal suggested that the Atkins Diet is more beneficial than previously thought. In both studies, for example, subjects who used a low-carbohydrate diet increased their high-density lipoproteins (the "good cholesterol") and decreased their triglycerides more than subjects who used a low-fat diet. (Elevated levels of triglycerides are associated with a greater risk of heart disease.)

Because this information is as surprising as it is tantalizing, the two studies demand greater scrutiny. Consider the following:

- Both studies had very high dropout rates. Of the 195 subjects in the beginning of the studies, only 116 completed the programs – a dropout rate of about 40.5%.
- Both of these studies involved obese and severely obese subjects, the results of which may not be relevant to athletic populations.

- Both studies were short-term (one was six months and the other one year).
- Technically, only one of the studies specifically used the Atkins Diet (the year-long study). In the other study, the subjects used a "carbohydrate-restricted (low-carbohydrate) diet" which certainly resembles the Atkins Diet but the term "Atkins Diet" was not mentioned or discussed by the researchers.
- Both studies involved very minimal supervision of the subjects which may have had an enormous impact on the results. For example, subjects in the six-month study received dietary instruction but it was up to them to follow the guidelines. In this study, the subjects in the low-carbohydrate group were told to "restrict carbohydrate intake to 30 [grams] per day or less"; the subjects in the low-fat group were told to restrict their calories so that it was "sufficient to create a deficit of 500 calories per day." In the year-long study, subjects who used the low-carbohydrate diet were given a copy of *Dr. Atkins' New Diet Revolution* and were told to "read the book and follow the diet as described"; subjects who used the low-fat diet were given a copy of *The LEARN Program for Weight Management* and told to "read the manual and follow the program as described." The gross lack of supervision raises a specter of uncertainty as to how closely the subjects followed their assigned protocols or even if they followed them at all.
- In the six-month study, data for the caloric intakes and the percentages of carbohydrates, protein and fats that were consumed per day by the subjects were based upon their "dietary recall." Perhaps even more astonishing, *no data whatsoever* were provided as to the caloric intakes and the percentages of carbohydrates, protein and fats that were consumed by the subjects throughout the course of the one-year study. Neither of the two studies made any mention of the caloric expenditures of the subjects. It is quite possible that some of the subjects

participated in some type of activity that expedited their weight loss. Without having accurate data or controlling for caloric intake/expenditure and macronutrient consumption, the effectiveness of two diets cannot be compared. Indeed, who knows what the subjects actually consumed? These uncontrolled and unknown variables contaminate the scientific purity of the studies and make any results and conclusions highly suspect.

- Equally dubious is the fact that many of the analyses that were made by the researchers included data from *all of the subjects*. For the subjects who dropped out of the studies – a whopping 40.5% of the original subjects – their baseline values or last observed values were "carried forward." It is difficult to determine how the inclusion of data from individuals who did not complete the studies might have influenced the results and conclusions of the research.

- Assuming for the moment that the caloric intake of the subjects in the six-month study is accurate, the group who used the low-carbohydrate diet consumed an average of 189 less calories per day than the group who used the low-fat diet. This may not seem significant but done daily over the course of six months (182 days), it amounts to a difference of nearly 10 pounds. In other words, the greater loss of weight that was experienced by the subjects who used the low-carbohydrate diet may have been the result of consuming fewer calories, not fewer carbohydrates.

- In the six-month study, the subjects who used the low-carbohydrate diet decreased their weight and triglycerides more than the subjects who used the low-fat diet. However, the authors noted that "it is unclear whether these benefits of a carbohydrate-restricted diet extend beyond six months."

- In the year-long study, the subjects who used the Atkins Diet lost more weight than the subjects who used the high-carbohydrate, low-fat diet for the first six months.

However, the subjects who used the Atkins Diet began regaining weight after six months and eventually regained more weight than the subjects on the high-carbohydrate, low-fat diet. By the end of the year, there were no significant differences in weight loss between the groups.

- In the year-long study, the researchers noted that "long-term adherence to the low-carbohydrate Atkins diet may be difficult."

Be aware that the Atkins Diet has several caveats. First, most of the initial weight loss is water, not fat. Second, it is very structured and strict with limited food choices thereby making it difficult to maintain. Third, any diet that is based upon a low intake of carbohydrates is also low in fruits, vegetables and whole-grain products. Four, the diet is high in meat, butter, cheese, saturated fat and other artery cloggers which is very unhealthy. Five, the long-term safety and effectiveness of the diet are unknown.

A final point: One of the foundations of the Atkins Diet is that high-glycemic foods increase blood-insulin levels which lowers blood glucose (sugar). While this is true, there is no evidence that this hormonal reaction causes you to gain weight. Understand that any weight loss that is produced by the Atkins diet is because of a reduction in the amount of calories, not a reduction in the amount of carbohydrates. You can lose weight with any diet as long as the calories that you consume are less than the calories that you need.

THE ZONE DIET

Invented and promoted by Dr. Barry Sears, the Zone Diet calls for a food intake that consists of 40% carbohydrate, 30% protein and 30% fat. There is very little scientific evidence that the Zone Diet is more effective than other diets. In one study, subjects were randomly assigned to one of two diets that provided 1,200 calories per day. One group followed the Zone Diet and the other a "traditional" diet that consisted of 65% carbohydrate, 15% protein and 25% fat. After six weeks, both groups had similar losses of bodyweight and body fat. The fact of the matter is that any weight loss experienced from the Zone Diet – or any other diet, for that matter – is the result of caloric restriction.

With that said, there are a number of concerns with the Zone Diet. For one thing, following the diet does not allow for the intake of a variety of foods that are required to meet nutritional needs. Rather, the Zone Diet – similar to the Atkins Diet – calls for the consumption of a high amount of protein and fats. To achieve this, you must decrease your intake of carbohydrates. Doing so restricts the intake of healthy foods – such as fruits, vegetables and whole-grain products – which may lead to vitamin and mineral deficiencies. Since fewer carbohydrates are available as a source of energy, you will also fatigue more quickly during physical activities. Yes, it is true that many successful athletes have used the Zone Diet. But they were already successful *before* they used it.

More importantly, however, the Zone Diet poses significant health risks. The National Research Council recommends against consuming protein in amounts greater than twice the Recommended Dietary Allowances because high intakes are associated with certain cancers and heart disease. A high intake of fat is also associated with heart disease. Consider this: In the aforementioned study, the group that used the "traditional" diet had a decrease in triglycerides while the group that used the Zone Diet had an increase. In addition, a high intake of protein increases the levels of uric acid which may cause gout in those who are susceptible. Excreting an excessive amount of protein stresses the liver and kidneys. There are additional concerns as well.

Chapter 20

FIVE FACTS ABOUT FAT

In order to compete at an optimal level, you should strive to maintain a desirable amount of body fat (or adipose tissue). Indeed, having too much body fat can adversely affect your performance on the mat.

There are several misconceptions about body fat. Understanding the facts about fat will help you to plot an effective course of action to keep it at desirable levels.

FAT FACT #1: Fat has several important functions.

While muscle cells are very active, fat cells are very inactive. Nevertheless, body fat does have a few important functions. First, fat serves as a major source of energy during low-intensity activities such as sleeping, reading and walking. Second, it helps in the transportation and absorption of fat-soluble vitamins (namely, vitamins A, D, E and K). Third, fat cushions impact and protects vital organs. Four, it provides insulation in cold weather. Be that as it may, having too much body fat is not really beneficial for athletes. In fact, there are probably only two activities in which an athlete would gain an advantage from having an excessive amount of body fat. One is long-distance swimming in cold water . . . and it would be swimming a very long distance in very cold water. The other is Sumo wrestling. So, having a high percentage of body fat is not desirable – unless, of course, you plan on swimming the English Channel (in January) or competing against a yokozuna in Japan.

FAT FACT #2: Fat is located throughout the body in different storage sites.

There are two main categories of fat deposition: essential

and storage. Essential fat is stored in your muscles, central nervous system and vital organs such as your heart, lungs, kidneys and liver. In addition, essential fat includes gender-specific fat such as that found in a woman's hips, thighs and breasts. For the most part, gender-specific fat is used during pregnancy and breastfeeding. Storage fat consists of subcutaneous fat and visceral fat. Subcutaneous fat lies in relatively small amounts directly underneath your skin; visceral fat is more internal and is used to cushion impact and protect vital organs.

Individuals tend to deposit fat in certain areas of their bodies more than in other areas. The reason for this is because the accumulation of fat is an inherited characteristic just like the color of your eyes, the shape of your nose and the distribution of your hair. When it comes to storing fat, people are very similar to their ancestors. So if your ancestors tended to deposit fat in their abdominal areas, it is likely that you will as well. Although there are individual differences, a male tends to store fat in his mid-section and upper back; a female tends to store fat in her hips and thighs.

Also consider this: Fat is lost in the reverse order in which it is deposited. In other words, if you have a tendency to deposit fat first on your arms and then on your legs, you will lose fat first from your legs and then from your arms.

FAT FACT #3: Fat does not turn into muscle.

It is a fairly common belief that you can change fat into muscle. In truth, you cannot change fat into muscle – or vice versa – any more than you can change lead into gold. Adipose tissue is composed of spherical cells that are specifically designed to store fat. It is about 22% water, 6% protein and 72% fat. Conversely, muscle tissue consists of special contractile proteins that allow movement to occur. Muscle tissue is about 70% water, 22% protein and 7% fat. (The remaining 1% or so includes inorganic salts such as calcium, potassium and sodium.) Since muscle and fat are two different and distinct types of biological tissue, fat cannot turn into muscle if you begin lifting weights (or doing any other type of physical activity); similarly, muscle cannot turn into fat if you stop lifting weights. The fact is that muscles hypertrophy (or become larger) from physical activity and muscles atrophy (or become smaller) from physical inactivity.

FAT FACT #4: Fat cannot be selectively reduced from specific areas of your body.

In exercise-physiology parlance, the belief that exercise causes a localized loss of body fat is known as "spot reduction." A litmus test for evaluating the notion of spot reduction is to examine whether a significantly greater change occurs in an active or exercised body part compared to a relatively inactive or unexercised body part. In one study, researchers evaluated the effects of a 27-day sit-up program on the fat-cell diameter and body composition of 13 subjects. Over this four-week period, each subject performed a total of 5,004 sit-ups (with the legs bent at a 90-degree angle and no foot support). Fat biopsies from the abdominal, subscapular and gluteal sites revealed that the sit-up program reduced the fat-cell diameter at all three sites to a similar degree. If spot reduction was possible, exercising the abdominal muscles would have preferentially decreased the fat in the abdominal area more than the gluteal or subscapular areas.

While on the subject, the abdominal area probably gets more attention than any other body part. Many individuals perform countless repetitions of sit-ups, crunches, side bends, torso twists, knee-ups and other abdominal exercises – sometimes more than once per day – with the belief that this will give them a highly prized set of "washboard abs." It is important to realize that everyone has "washboard abs." But whether or not these muscles are seen depends upon the thickness of the fat that covers the abdominal area. If your abdominal area has a low amount of fat, your "abs" will appear very defined or "toned"; if your abdominal area has a high amount of fat, your "abs" will not appear very defined or "toned." This does not mean that your abdominal muscles are not developed. Rather, they are camouflaged with a pesky layer of fat. Abdominal exercises certainly involve your abdominal muscles. However, the exercises have little effect on the subcutaneous fat that resides below your skin and over your abdominal muscles. Years ago, I knew one well-meaning individual – a former professional wrestler – who regularly performed 1,500 crunches during each workout, yet he looked as if he just swallowed a Volkswagen! The reason why you cannot selectively lose fat from a specific area is that when you exercise, fat (and carbohydrate) stores are tapped from throughout your body as a source of energy – not just from one specific area. So, you can do abdominal exercises until the sun runs out of fuel and explodes – about five billion years from now – but these Olympian efforts will not automatically trim your mid-section. Quite simply, spot reduction is physiologically impossible.

Your abdominals should be treated like any other muscle group. Once an activity for your abdominals exceeds about 70 seconds in duration, it becomes an increasingly greater test of aerobic endurance instead of muscular strength. Your abdominals can be targeted effectively in a time-efficient manner by training them to the point of muscular fatigue within about 8 - 12 repetitions (or about 50 - 70 seconds).

FAT FACT #5: Fat is not decreased significantly if weight is lost too rapidly.

Losing weight is a simple matter of mathematics. To lose weight, you must produce a caloric deficit: You must expend more calories than you consume. Actually, you can achieve a caloric deficit by decreasing your caloric consumption (eating less), increasing your caloric expenditure (exercising more) or a combination of the two. In fact, proper weight loss should be a blend of consuming less calories and expending more calories.

Understand that the rate at which you lose weight determines how much of the caloric expenditure actually came from fat. The daily caloric deficit should not be more than about 500 - 1,000 calories below the normal daily needs. If the weight loss is more than about 1% of your bodyweight per week, it is likely that some of this weight reduction will be the result of decreased lean-body mass and/or water rather than body fat.

However, if the weight loss is less than about 1% of your bodyweight per week and is the result of a rigorous training program in conjunction with a reduced caloric intake, then it will probably be in the form of decreased body fat.

So, losing weight too rapidly is not very desirable . . . nor is it very healthy. Keep this in mind when you are trying to lose weight and fat.

FACE THE FACTS

Remember that in order to wrestle at your best, you should not carry too much body fat. You can increase the likelihood that you will achieve a desirable level of body fat by following a realistic approach that is based upon the facts about fat.

Chapter 21
STRENGTH AND FITNESS
ON THE WEB

In October 1990, Tim Berners-Lee coined the term "World Wide Web." Born as we know it roughly one year later, the "web" offers coaches and athletes an incredible amount of information that is accurate and worthwhile. Equally incredible, however, is the amount of information that is inaccurate and worthless.

WEB SITE-INGS

Wrestling coaches and their athletes can obtain excellent information on virtually all aspects of strength and fitness from the following 12 web sites (presented in alphabetical order):

1. www.cyberpump.com. This award-winning site has been in existence since 1995, making it one of the oldest strength-training sites on the web. It is maintained by a former competitive powerlifter (who at one time was one of the top 50 deadlifters in the United States in the 198-pound class, doing a 600-pound deadlift in competition). The site is extremely popular among strength enthusiasts and has been mentioned in numerous magazines – ranging from *U. S. News and World Report* to *GQ* – and several books. Described as "the Home of HIT (High Intensity Training)," this site contains an unbelievable amount of information that has been contributed by an impressive array of strength-training authorities (such as Dr. Ken Leistner, Stuart McRobert and Dr. Richard Winett) and strength coaches (such as Ken Mannie of Michigan State University). Besides providing advice on strength training and nutrition, the

116

site contains five active Q&A sections (with an archive of nearly 10,000 previous questions and answers) as well as video and audio clips. Two specialty sub-sites are offered on it (TotalCoaching.com and GripPage.com) along with two discussion forums (the Garage Gym and GripBoard). Finally, the site announces upcoming strength-training seminars/clinics and book releases.

2. www.fitness.gov. From The President's Council on Physical Fitness and Sports, this site provides an abundance of basic but useful information on exercise, physical activity, health and nutrition. The site offers research and resources for coaches and teachers. In particular, it is an excellent resource for wrestling coaches who may also be physical educators.

3. www.fitnessmanagement.com. This site is from *Fitness Management* magazine, a leading publication for fitness professionals. It contains hundreds of archived articles (from the magazine) on a wide variety of topics such as flexibility, strength training, motivation and nutrition.

4. www.gssiweb.com. From the Gatorade Sports Science Institute, this site includes a sports science center that offers information which is scientific as well as practical. Topics of interest to coaches and wrestlers include those on hydration and supplements.

5. www.i-a-r-t.com. This site boasts articles on training, nutrition and sports. It is maintained by Brian Johnston, co-founder and president of the International Association of Resistance Trainers (an educational institute offering certifications and resources in exercise and nutrition science). He is also a creative and thought-provoking author of books and articles on strength and fitness.

6. www.integrativehealthcare.com. Coaches and wrestlers will find some great information on a wide variety of topics on this site. It offers many articles (on such areas as athletes, ergogenics and the glycemic index) and several online tools, including a diet analysis which "lets

you enter the foods you've eaten for one day and then reports a complete nutritional review of your diet based on the Recommended Dietary Allowances [RDAs] for your demographic." Specifically, the tool will analyze your intakes of calories (energy), protein, Vitamin A, Vitamin C, several B Vitamins (thiamin, riboflavin, niacin, B-6, folate and B-12) and minerals (calcium, phosphorus, magnesium, iron and zinc) as a percentage of the RDA. This is an extremely detailed analysis, by the way. For example, the category of "beverages" lists 181 different foods.

7. www.nat.uiuc.edu. This is an excellent educational site that is kept by the Department of Food Science and Human Nutrition at the University of Illinois at Urbana-Champaign. It has an "energy calculator" which you can use to determine how many calories that you expend during the course of the day. Additionally, the site contains several educational resources (such as information on sports nutrition and soy) and a calculator to estimate your percentage of body fat (although you will need access to skinfold calipers). There is also a nutritional analysis tool on this site.

8. www.naturalstrength.com. This site is maintained by Bob Whelan, a strength coach in the Washington, D. C. area. It contains a huge inventory of articles written by numerous collegiate strength coaches (such as Ken Mannie, Aaron Hillman and Fred Cantor), scholastic strength coaches (such as Marty Gasparro) and strength enthusiasts (such as Jan Dellinger, a former long-time employee of the legendary York Barbell Company). There are also many nutrition articles on the site, including at least three dozen by Nancy Clark, a nutritional authority and famous author. Finally, the site has a "store" where you can purchase audio- and videotapes. (The videotapes are of presentations made by various speakers at annual conferences that have been hosted by Coach Whelan.)

9. www.quackwatch.com. This site contains loads of information on "health fraud, quackery and intelligent decisions." It is operated by Stephen Barret, M.D., who is an author, editor and consumer advocate. According to the site, its purpose is to "combat health-related frauds, myths, fads and fallacies." Among other things, the site contains features and consumer strategies and discusses questionable advertisements. Specific topics of interest to coaches and wrestlers include information on calorie blockers, cellulite removers, dietary supplements, ergogenic aids, gamma hydroxybutyrate (GHB), dehydroepiandrosterone (DHEA) and "weight control gimmicks and frauds."

10. www-rohan.sdsu.edu/dept/coachsci/index. This site is not for everyone but it is quite informative nonetheless, particularly for those who are interested in research. You can find literally hundreds of research abstracts on a wide range of topics, including principles of training, specificity of training, positive mental activity, measuring practice effort, strength training, goal-setting, fuel and ergogenic aids, the young athlete, psychological dynamics of performance, coaching factors and mental factors in sports.

11. www.strongerathlete.com. Since 1995, Coach Jeff Roudebush of Truman High School (Independence, Missouri) has been training his athletes with a program that incorporates safe, efficient methods. Frustrated by the widespread use of programs in the Kansas City area that use dangerous, inefficient methods, he and Coach Sam Knopik created this site to "get out the word." According to the site, its purpose is "to promote safe, productive, and efficient methods of strength training for high school and collegiate athletes while debunking the Olympic lifting establishment that has engulfed many of our high school and college athletic programs." In addition, their desire is "to create better athletes through controlled and intense strength training."

12. www.thedietchannel.com. This site provides an as-

tounding 600 links to reliable diet information (on such topics as weight loss, fad diets, diet pills, sports nutrition and sports supplements). Using the tools on the site, you can analyze your diet and food intake; your caloric needs; your fat, protein and carbohydrate needs; the number of calories you "burn" during exercise; your body-mass index (BMI); and the fat or sodium content of your foods. The site also contains numerous articles, including ones on successful weight-loss tips, nutritional energy drinks and nutrition quackery.

WEB OF KNOWLEDGE

The amount of useful information that is available on the web is truly staggering. Applying the knowledge from the web can help you realize your potential as a wrestler. And just think: The information is only a few clicks away!

Disclaimer: The information that is contained in this chapter was accurate at the time that it was written. Understand, however, that the web is a constantly evolving entity and the information – and web-site addresses – may change or even disappear.

BIBLIOGRAPHY

The following articles from *Wrestling USA* magazine (call 406-549-4448) were reprinted as chapters in this book:

- Basic Training for Wrestling: The Essentials. vol 37, no 4 (November 15, 2001): 6-7.
- Factors that Determine Strength Potential. vol 38, no 10 (April 15, 2003): 6, 8-10.
- How Many Sets? vol 39, no 3 (October 15, 2003): 6-7
- Post-Fatigue Repetitions. vol 37, no 3 (October 15, 2001): 60-61.
- Five Steps for Productive Reps. vol 38, no 8 (March 1, 2003): 6-8.
- Order of Exercise Essential for Producing Optimal Improvement. vol 37, no 2 (October 1, 2001): 12-14.
- The Importance of Recovery. vol 39, no 4 (November 15, 2003): 6-7.
- Documenting Your Performance in the Weight Room. vol 38, no 7 (February 15, 2003): 6-7.
- Improving Power for Wrestling. vol 37, no 5 (December 15, 2001): 6-7.
- Back with a Vengeance. vol 38, no 3 (October 15, 2002): 6-8.
- A Grip Tip. vol 38, no 2 (October 1, 2002): 6.
- Which are Better: Free Weights or Machines? vol 38, no 4 (November 15, 2002): 6-8.
- Dumbbell Training. vol 39 no 2 (October 1, 2003): 6-8.
- Wrestling Camp 2002 Q&A on Strength and Conditioning. vol 38, no 5 (December 15, 2002): 10-1

- Perspectives on Periodization and Plyometrics. vol 38, no 9 (March 15, 2003): 6, 8-9.
- Caloric Contributions and Needs. vol 37, no 8 (March 1, 2002): 6-7.
- Pre- and Post-Activity Foods/Fuels. vol 37, no 7 (February 15, 2002): 6-7.
- Nutritional Questions & Answers. vol 39, no 1 (September 15, 2003): 6-8.
- Fad Diets: Atkins and Zone. vol 39, no 6 (January 15, 2004): 6-8.
- Five Facts about Fat. vol 39, no 7 (February 15, 2004): 6-7.
- Strength and Fitness on the Web. vol 38, no 1 (September 15, 2002): 6-7.

BIOGRAPHY

Matt Brzycki enlisted in the United States Marine Corps in June 1975. His active duty began two months later when he was sent to basic training (a.k.a. "boot camp") in Parris Island, South Carolina. When Mr. Brzycki completed his basic training in November 1975, he was presented the Leatherneck Award for achieving the highest score in rifle marksmanship in his platoon. In January 1978 – a little more than 28 months after beginning basic training – he was promoted meritoriously to the rank of sergeant. In May 1978, Mr. Brzycki entered Drill Instructor (DI) School at the Marine Corps Recruit Depot in San Diego, California. When he graduated from the school in August 1978 at the age of 21, he was one of the youngest DIs in the entire Marine Corps. Among his many responsibilities as a DI was the physical preparedness of Marine recruits. In August 1979, Mr. Brzycki was awarded a Certificate of Merit for successfully completing a tour of duty as a DI.

Shortly after his four-year enlistment ended in August 1979, Mr. Brzycki enrolled at Penn State. He earned a Bachelor of Science degree in Health and Physical Education in May 1983. Mr. Brzycki represented the university for two years in the Pennsylvania State Collegiate Powerlifting Championships (1981 and 1982) and was also a place-winner in his first bodybuilding competition (1981).

From May 1983 - August 1984, Mr. Brzycki served as a Health Fitness Supervisor at Princeton University. In September 1984, he was named the Assistant Strength and Conditioning Coach at Rutgers University and remained in that position until July 1990. In August 1990, he returned to Princeton

University as the school's Strength Coach and Health Fitness Coordinator. Mr. Brzycki was named the Coordinator of Health Fitness, Strength and Conditioning Programs in February 1994 (retroactive to December 1993). In March 2001, he was named the Coordinator of Recreational Fitness and Wellness Programming.

Over the years, Mr. Brzycki has worked with literally hundreds of male and female athletes in a wide variety of sports. Since November 1982, he has been involved in the strength and conditioning of collegiate wrestlers at three different schools: Penn State, Princeton and Rutgers.

Mr. Brzycki has taught at the collegiate level since 1990. He developed the Strength Training Theory and Applications course for Exercise Science and Sports Studies majors at Rutgers University and taught the program from March 1990 - July 2000 as a member of the Faculty of Arts and Sciences. (Department of Exercise Science and Sport Studies.) He also taught the same course to Health and Physical Education majors at The College of New Jersey from January 1996 - March 1999 as a member of the Health and Physical Education Faculty. All told, more than 600 university students in fitness-related majors took his courses in strength training for academic credit. Since September 1990, Mr. Brzycki has taught non-credit physical education courses at Princeton University including all of those pertaining to weight training.

Mr. Brzycki has been a featured speaker at local, regional, state and national conferences, clinics and camps throughout the United States and Canada. Since November 1984, he has written more than 240 articles on strength and fitness that have been featured in 40 different publications. Mr. Brzycki has written five books: *A Practical Approach to Strength Training* (1995), *Youth Strength and Conditioning* (1995), *Cross Training for Fitness* (1997), *Wrestling Strength: The Competitive Edge* (2002) and *Wrestling Strength: Prepare to Win* (2002). He has also co-authored four books: *Conditioning for Basketball* (1993), *SWAT Fitness* (2003), *Conditioning for Baseball* (2003) and *The Female Athlete: Train for Success* (2004). Mr. Brzycki served as the editor of *Maximize your Training: Insights from Leading Strength and Fitness Professionals* (1999). This 448-page book features the collective efforts of 37 leaders in the strength and fitness profession. In 1997, he developed a correspondence course in strength training for Desert Southwest Fitness (Tucson, Arizona) that is used by strength and fitness professionals to update their certifications. The course has been approved and accepted for continuing education credits by 16 international organizations including the American Council on Exercise, the Australian Fitness Advisory Council, the International Fitness Professionals Association, the International Weightlifting Association and the National Federation of Professional Trainers.

In January 2001, Mr. Brzycki was named a Fellow at Forbes College (Princeton University). In April 2001, he was selected to serve on the Alumni Society Board of Directors for the College of Health & Human Development (Penn State). He and his wife, Alicia, reside in Lawrenceville, New Jersey, with their son, Ryan.

Also available by Matt Brzycki:

Wrestling Strength: The Competitive Edge
ISBN: 0-9718959-0-2 • $12.95 • 128 pages • 5½ x 8½
Topics covered include:

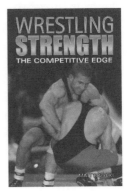

- Conventional Strength Training
- A Practical Approach
- The "Twenty-Hour Rule": A Strength Coach's Perspective
- Designing a Strength Program
- Stimulating Muscular Growth
- Fiber Types and Repetition Ranges
- Vary Your Workouts
- Metabolic Conditioning
- The Pre-Exhaustion Principle: Bypassing the Weak Link
- Getting the Most Out of Dips and Chins
- Manual Resistance for Wrestlers
- More Manual Resistance
- Get a Grip!

And much, much more!

Wrestling Strength: Prepare to Win
ISBN: 0-9718959-1-0 • $12.95 • 128 pages • 5½ x 8½
Topics covered include:

- Strength Training: Set Your Priorities!
- Injury Trends in Wrestling
- Protecting the Knee
- Protecting the Shoulder
- Rehabilitative Strength Training
- The Importance of Intensity
- The Importance of Progressive Overload
- New Perspectives in Strength
- Ten Myths in Strength and Fitness
- Coach, I Wanna Be Explosive!
- Adolescent Strength Training
- The Trap Bar: A Productive Alternative
- Strengthening the Abdominals

And much, much more!

*Available in quality bookstores everywhere or by calling
(800) 296-0481. Or visit our distributor's website:*

www.cardinalpub.com